P9-DCH-464

Trees of Minnesota
Field Guide

by Stan Tekiela

Adventure Publications, Inc.
Cambridge, Minnesota

*To my wife Katherine and
daughter Abigail with all my love*

ACKNOWLEDGMENTS

Special thanks to John D. Jackson, Ph.D., Rick Klevorn, Stuart A. Fox, and Jeff Cordes for their help with this book, and Janet R. Larson for her knowledge of conifers. Special thanks also to Sandy Livoti for her exceptional eye to detail.

Book design and leaf illustrations by Jonathan Norberg

Tree illustrations by Julie Martinez

Photo credits by photographer and page number:

Cover photo: Aspens by Stan Tekiela

Dembinsky Photo Associates: 50 (fruit), 70 (fruit), 130 (flower), 162 (all), 164 (fruit) **Dudley Edmondson**: 4 (all), 16 (all), 32 (needle), 36 (leaf, bark, flower), 44 (leaf), 50 (flower), 54 (both), 56 (fruit), 72 (flower), 74 (all), 80 (all), 94 (all), 108 (fruit), 114 (leaf, fruit), 122 (all), 128 (fruit), 130 (fruit), 140 (bark), 144 (flower, fruit), 160 (flower), 164 (bark), 166 (bark, fruit), 168 (bark) **Stan Tekiela**: all other photos

TABLE OF CONTENTS

MINNESOTA AND TREES

Minnesota is a great place for anyone interested in trees. With *Trees of Minnesota Field Guide*, you'll be able to quickly identify 93 of the most common trees in Minnesota—nearly all of which are native to the state. This guide also includes a number of common non-native trees that have been naturalized in Minnesota. This book makes no attempt to identify cultivated or nursery trees.

Because this book is a unique all-photographic guide just for Minnesota, you won't have to page through photographs of trees that don't grow in our state, or attempt to identify live trees by studying black-and-white line drawings.

Trees of Minnesota Field Guide is the third in a series of very unique field guides, with *Birds of Minnesota Field Guide* and *Wildflowers of Minnesota Field Guide* paving the way to this new means of understanding nature.

WHAT IS A TREE?

For the purposes of this book, a tree is defined as a large woody perennial plant, usually with a single erect trunk, standing at least 15 feet (4.5 m) tall, with a well-defined crown. *Trees of Minnesota Field Guide* helps you observe some basic characteristics of trees so you can identify different species confidently.

HOW THIS BOOK IS ORGANIZED

To identify a tree, you'll want to start by looking at the thumb tab in the upper right-hand corner of the text pages. These thumb tabs define the sections of the book. The tab combines several identifying features of a tree (main category, needle or leaf type and attachment) into one icon.

It's possible to identify trees using this field guide without learning about categories, leaf types and attachments. Simply flip through the pages to match your sample to the features depicted on the thumb tabs. Once you find the correct section, use the photos to find your tree. Or, you may want to learn more about the features of trees in a methodical way, using the following steps to narrow your choices to just a few photos.

1. First, determine the appropriate section and find the right icon by asking these questions: Is the tree a conifer, or is it deciduous? If it's a conifer, are the needles single, clustered or scaly? If it's deciduous, is the leaf type simple, lobed or compound, and do leaves attach to twigs in an opposite or alternate pattern?

2. Next, simply browse through the photos in that section to find your tree. Or, to further narrow your choices, use the icon in the lower right-hand corner of the text pages. These icons are grouped by the general shape of the needle or leaf, and increase in size as the average size of the needle or leaf increases.

3. Finally, by examining the full-page photos of needles or leaves, studying inset photos of bark, flowers, fruit or other special features and considering the information on text pages, you should be able to confidently identify the tree.

While these steps briefly summarize how you can use this book, it is quite helpful to learn more about how the sections are grouped by reading the Identification Step-by-Step section.

IDENTIFICATION STEP-BY-STEP
Conifer or Deciduous

Trees in this field guide are first grouped into two main categories that consist of 16 conifer trees and 77 deciduous trees.

Trees with evergreen needles that remain on branches year-round and have seeds in cones are conifers. Some examples of these are pines and spruces. The only exception in this main category is the Tamarack, a conifer that behaves like a deciduous tree, shedding its needles in autumn. Trees with broad flat leaves that fall off their branches each autumn are deciduous. Some examples of these are oaks and maples.

You will see by looking at the thumb tabs that trees with needles (conifers) are shown in the first sections of the book, followed by trees with leaves (deciduous).

Needle or Leaf Type

CONIFER GROUP: SINGLE, CLUSTERED OR SCALY NEEDLES

SINGLE   **CLUSTERED**   **SCALY**
(RANGE OF 2-30 NEEDLES)

If the tree is a conifer, the next step is to distinguish among single, clustered and scaly needles. Begin by checking the number of needles that arise from one point. If you see only one needle arising from one point, look in the single needle section. Conifers with single needles are shown first. If there are at least two needles arising from one point, turn to the clustered needles section. This second section is organized by the number of needles in a cluster. If you are trying to identify needles that overlap each other and have a scale-like appearance unlike the other needles, you will find this type in the scaly needles section.

DECIDUOUS GROUP: SIMPLE, LOBED OR COMPOUND

SIMPLE   **LOBED**   **COMPOUND**   **TWICE COMPOUND**   **PALMATE COMPOUND**

If the tree is deciduous, the next step is to determine the leaf type. Many of the simple leaves have a basic shape such as oval, round or triangular. Other simple leaves are lobed, identified by noticeable indentations along their edges. Simple leaves without lobes are grouped first, followed by the lobed leaf groups.

If a leaf is composed of smaller leaflets growing along a single stalk, you'll find this type in the compound leaf sections. When a leaf has small leaflets growing along the edge of a thinner secondary stalk, which is in turn attached to a thicker main stalk, check the twice compound section. If the leaf has leaflets emerging from a common central point at the end of a leafstalk, look in the palmate compound section.

Leaf Attachment

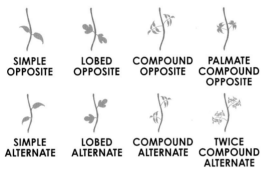

SIMPLE
OPPOSITE

LOBED
OPPOSITE

COMPOUND
OPPOSITE

PALMATE
COMPOUND
OPPOSITE

SIMPLE
ALTERNATE

LOBED
ALTERNATE

COMPOUND
ALTERNATE

TWICE
COMPOUND
ALTERNATE

For deciduous trees, once you have determined the appropriate leaf type, give special attention to the pattern in which the leaves are attached to the twig. Trees with leaves that attach directly opposite of each other on a twig are grouped first in each section, followed by trees with leaves that attach alternately. The thumb tabs are labeled "opposite" or "alternate" to reflect the attachment group. All the above features (main category, needle or leaf type and attachment) are depicted in one icon for easy use.

Needle or Leaf Size

Once you have found the correct section by using the thumb tabs, note that the section is further loosely organized by needle or leaf size from small to large. Size is depicted in the needle or leaf icon located in the lower right-hand corner of text pages. This icon also reflects the shape of the needle or leaf. For example, the icon for the Amur Maple, which has a leaf size of 2-4", is smaller than the icon for the Norway Maple with a leaf size of 5-7". Measurement of any deciduous leaf extends from the base of the leaf (excluding the leafstalk) to the tip.

Using Photos and Icons to Confirm the Identify

After using the thumb tabs to narrow your choices, the last step is to confirm the tree's identity. First, compare the full-page photo of the leaves and twigs to be sure they look similar. Next, study the color and texture of the bark, and compare it to the inset photo. Then consider the information given about the habitat and range.

Sometimes, however, it is a special characteristic, such as flowers, fruit or thorns (described and/or pictured), that is an even better indicator of the identity. In general, if it's spring, check for flowers. During summer, look for fruit. In autumn, note the fall color.

Another icon is also included for each species to show the overall shape of the average mature tree, and how its height compares with a two-story house. For trees with an average height of more than 50 feet (15 m), this icon is shown on a slightly smaller scale.

STAN'S NOTES

Stan's Notes is fun and fact-filled with many gee-whiz tidbits of interesting information such as historical uses, other common names and much more. Most information given in this descriptive section cannot be found in other tree field guides.

CAUTION

In Stan's Notes, it's occasionally mentioned that parts of some trees were used for medicine or food. While some find this interesting, DO NOT use this field guide to identify edible or medicinal trees. Certain trees in the state have toxic properties or poisonous look-alikes that can cause severe problems. Do not take the chance of making a mistake. Please enjoy the trees of Minnesota with your eyes, nose or with your camera. In addition, please don't pull off leaves, cut branches or attempt to transplant any trees. Nearly all of the trees you will see are available at your local garden centers. These trees have been cultivated and have not been uprooted from the wild. Trees are an important part of our natural environment, and leaving a healthy tree unharmed will do a great deal to help keep our state the wondrous place it is.

Enjoy the Trees!

Stan

LEAF BASICS

It's easier to identify trees and communicate about them when you know the names of the different parts of a leaf. For instance, it is more effective to use the word "sinus" to indicate an indentation on an edge of a leaf than to try to describe it.

The following illustrations show conifer needles in cross section and basic parts of deciduous leaves. The simple/lobed and compound leaf illustrations are composites of leaves and should not be confused with any actual leaf of a real tree.

Needle Cross Sections

square   flat   triangular   round

Simple/Lobed Leaf

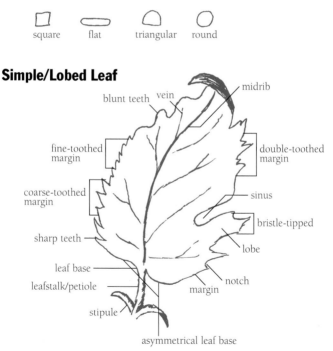

midrib
blunt teeth   vein
fine-toothed margin
double-toothed margin
coarse-toothed margin
sinus
bristle-tipped
sharp teeth
lobe
leaf base
leafstalk/petiole
notch
margin
stipule
asymmetrical leaf base

Compound Leaf

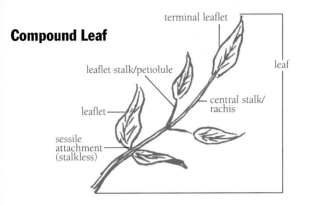

terminal leaflet

leaflet stalk/petiolule

leaflet

sessile attachment (stalkless)

central stalk/ rachis

leaf

FINDING YOUR TREE IN A SECTION

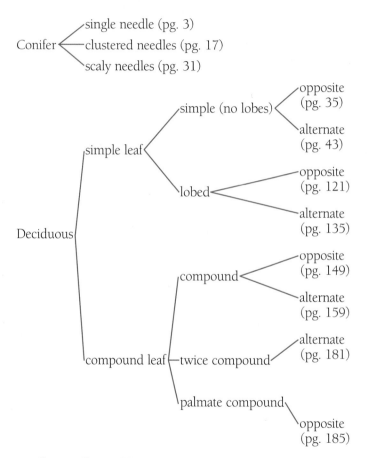

Conifer
— single needle (pg. 3)
— clustered needles (pg. 17)
— scaly needles (pg. 31)

Deciduous

simple leaf
— simple (no lobes)
  — opposite (pg. 35)
  — alternate (pg. 43)
— lobed
  — opposite (pg. 121)
  — alternate (pg. 135)

compound leaf
— compound
  — opposite (pg. 149)
  — alternate (pg. 159)
— twice compound
  — alternate (pg. 181)
— palmate compound
  — opposite (pg. 185)

Smaller needles and leaves tend to be toward the front of each section, while larger sizes can be found toward the back. Check the icon in the lower right corner of text pages to compare relative size.

COMMON NAME
Scientific name

Family: common family name (scientific family name)

Height: average range in feet and meters of the mature tree from ground to top of crown

Tree: overall description, may include a shape, type of trunk, branches or crown

Leaf/Needle: type of leaf or needle, shape, size and attachment, may include lobes, leaflets, margin, veins, color or leafstalk

Bark: color and texture of the trunk, may include inner bark or thorns

Flower: catkin, flower, may include shape, size or color

Fruit/Cone: seed, nut, berry, may include shape, size or color

Fall Color: color(s) that deciduous leaves turn to in autumn

Origin/Age: native or non-native to the state; average life span

Habitat: type of soil, places found, sun or shade tolerance

Range: throughout or part of Minnesota where the tree is found, may include places where planted

Stan's Notes: Helpful identification information, history, origin and other interesting gee-whiz nature facts.

Shape of an individual needle, needle cluster or leaf. Use this icon to compare relative size among similarly shaped leaves.

BARK

CONE

CLOSE-UP

WHITE SPRUCE
Picea glauca

Family: Pine (Pinaceae)

Height: 40-60' (12-18 m)

Tree: single straight trunk, many horizontal branches sometimes sloping down, ragged conical crown

Needle: single needle, ⅓-¾" (.8-2 cm) long, stiff, pointed, square in cross section, aromatic when crushed, bluish green with a line of white dots on all sides

Bark: light gray in color, many flaky scales, inner bark is salmon pink

Cone: green, turning brown at maturity, smooth to the touch, 1-2½" (2.5-6 cm) long, single or in clusters, hanging from branch

Origin/Age: native; 175-200 years

Habitat: variety of soils, usually not as wet as Black Spruce (pg. 5) soils, often growing on banks of lakes and streams, sometimes in pure stands

Range: northern half of the state

Stan's Notes: Also known as Skunk Spruce because its crushed needles give off a strong odor that reminds some of skunk. Needles have a whitish cast, giving this tree its common name. Like all other species of spruce, White Spruce needles are square in cross section. Needles frequently last seven to ten years before falling off, leaving a raised base on the twig. Susceptible to fire and Spruce Budworm, a caterpillar that eats new needles. Lower branches die and fall off, leaving the trunk straight and lacking branches. A variety, Black Hills White Spruce (*P. glauca densata*) is a widely planted urban tree.

BARK

CONE

BLACK SPRUCE
Picea mariana

Family: Pine (Pinaceae)

Height: 25-50' (7.5-15 m)

Tree: small to medium-sized slender tree with a narrow pyramid shape, many dead lower branches, upper branches widely spread and drooping

Needle: single needle, ¼-1" (.6-2.5 cm) long, densely set along twig, straight, blunt-tipped, square in cross section, dull blue green

Bark: reddish brown in color, large scales, inner bark is olive green

Cone: lavender to purple, turning brown when mature, egg-shaped, ½-1½" (1-4 cm) long, hanging from the branch

Origin/Age: native; 150-200 years

Habitat: wet or poorly drained soils, bogs, peats, often in pure stands or with Tamarack (pg. 29)

Range: northeastern quarter of the state

Stan's Notes: Relatively slow-growing, long-lived tree that is found in the northeastern part of Minnesota. One of seven spruce species native to North America. Common along marshes and bogs, with cones usually occurring at the top of tree. Cones mature in autumn but often don't open, remaining on the tree for up to 15 years. Heat from fire opens the cones, after which many seeds are released. This species can live as long as 200 years, but obtains a height of only 50 feet (15 m). Young twigs have tiny orange-to-brown hairs. Treetops are commonly used in planters during winter for decoration. Long fibers in the wood make it desirable for making paper. A golden-colored pitch that collects on wounds was once gathered and sold as spruce gum.

BARK

ONE

COLORADO SPRUCE
Picea pungens

Family: Pine (Pinaceae)

Height: 40-60' (12-18 m)

Tree: pyramid shape, lower branches are the widest and often touch the ground

Needle: single needle, ½-1" (1-2.5 cm) long, very stiff, very sharp point on the end, square in cross section, bluish green to silver blue

Bark: grayish brown and flaky, becoming reddish brown and deeply furrowed with age

Cone: straw-colored, 2-4" (5-7.5 cm) long, in clusters or single, hanging down

Origin/Age: non-native, was introduced to the state from the Rocky Mountains; 150-200 years (some can reach 600 years in some western states)

Habitat: variety of soils, does best in clay and moist soils

Range: throughout, in cities, parks, along roads, planted around homes

Stan's Notes: A common Christmas tree and landscaping tree that is widely planted around homes and along city streets. Naturalized now throughout Minnesota. Victim of the Spruce Budworm and needle fungus, so not planted as much anymore. Very susceptible to cytospora canker, which invades stressed trees, causing loss of branches and eventual death. Will grow in a wide variety of soils, but prefers moist and well drained. Slow growing, some living up to 600 years in the West. Very sharp needles that are square in cross section. The species name refers to its pungent odor. Also known as Blue Spruce or Silver Spruce.

CONE

BARK

NORWAY SPRUCE
Picea abies

Family: Pine (Pinaceae)

Height: 50-70' (15-21 m)

Tree: pyramid shape, single trunk, branches drooping or weeping

Needle: single needle, ½-1" (1-2.5 cm) long, with a slight curve, stiff and pointed, square in cross section, aromatic when crushed, deep blue green

Bark: reddish gray, many round scales

Cone: straw brown, papery, 2-7" (5-18 cm) long, hangs from branch

Origin/Age: non-native, introduced to the U.S. from Europe and Asia; 150-200 years

Habitat: rich moist soils

Range: throughout, as windbreaks, in parks, cemeteries and yards

Stan's Notes: Produces the largest cones of all spruces. The fastest growing and tallest spruce in Minnesota, popular for planting as windbreaks. Introduced from Europe, as the name would imply, it is the dominant tree in the Black Forest area of Germany. One of the earliest trees used for reforestation in North America. The bark on the twigs is orange, turning reddish brown on the small branches. The trunk oozes a pitch known as burgundy pitch, which has been used in varnishes and medicine. Many horticultural varieties of this tree are available.

BARK

CONE

EASTERN HEMLOCK
Tsuga canadensis

Family: Pine (Pinaceae)

Height: 40-60' (12-18 m)

Tree: pyramid shape, spreading branches are horizontal with drooping tips, irregular crown

Needle: single needle, ½-1" (1-2.5 cm) long, arranged in 2 rows with a few shorter needles on the upper row, borne on a soft and flexible tan stalk, soft, flat, flexible, tapering at the end, dark yellow green above, lighter-colored with 2 whitish lengthwise parallel lines below

Bark: dark brown to dark gray in color, deeply grooved with broad flat-topped ridges

Cone: round to oval, ½-1" (1-2.5 cm) long, borne at the end of twig, hanging down

Origin/Age: native; 150-200 years (some reach 600 years)

Habitat: wet soils in cool moist sites, shade tolerant

Range: northeastern quarter of the state and isolated sites

Stan's Notes: One of four species of hemlock in the U.S. and the only one native to Minnesota. An extremely long-lived tree, some with trunk diameters measuring 4 feet (1 m). A very shade-tolerant tree, often growing in dense shade of taller trees, growing slowly until reaching the canopy. Because the tip of the leader shoot (treetop) droops, it often doesn't grow as straight as the other conifers. Bark is rich in tannic acid (tannin) and was once used to tan hides. Open cones will remain on the tree for up to two years. Has heavy seed crops every two to three years. Doesn't reproduce very well, as the young trees are fragile and often do not reach maturity. Doesn't transplant well. Also called Canada Hemlock.

BARK

CONE

BALSAM FIR
Abies balsamea

Family: Pine (Pinaceae)

Height: 50-75' (15-23 m)

Tree: tapering spire with horizontal branching from the ground up, dark green

Needle: single needle, ½-1" (1-2.5 cm) long, with a spiral arrangement on the twig, soft, flat, blunt-tipped, shiny green above, 2 silvery lengthwise lines or grooves below

Bark: light gray, smooth with many very aromatic raised resin blisters (pitch pockets), breaking with age and leaving brown scales

Cone: bluish, erect, 2-4" (5-10 cm) long, dense clusters near the top of tree

Origin/Age: native; 100-150 years

Habitat: moist soils, shaded forest, along bogs

Range: northern half of the state

Stan's Notes: Well known for its fragrant needles, this is a popular Christmas tree because it holds its needles well after cutting. One of 40 fir species worldwide. One of nine fir species in North America and one of only two species east of the Rocky Mountains, with the Fraser Fir (not shown) native to the Appalachian Mountains. Often attacked by the Spruce Budworm, which eats the new needles. The upright cones break apart by autumn, leaving only a thin central stalk. Resin from the trunk was once used for making varnishes and sealing birch bark canoes. The common name "Balsam" comes from the Greek root *balsamon*, which refers to aromatic oily resins found in the tree. Also called Canada Balsam or Eastern Fir.

IMMATURE
CONE

BARK

CONE

DOUGLAS-FIR
Pseudotsuga menziesii

Family: Pine (Pinaceae)

Height: 50-70' (15-21 m)

Tree: scraggly-looking tree, pyramid shape, many lower branches dead and remaining on the tree, open irregular crown

Needle: single needle, 1-1½" (2.5-4 cm) long, arranged spirally on a twig, borne from a raised stalk, soft, linear but often curved, sharp point on the end, flat in cross section, yellow green above, two lines of white dots below

Bark: gray to brown in color with many flaky scales and scattered resin blisters (pitch pockets)

Cone: green, turning brown to straw-colored at maturity, large and distinct, 2-4" (5-10 cm) long, with curly 3-pronged cone scales, hanging from branch

Origin/Age: non-native, introduced from the Rocky Mountains and Pacific Northwest; 150-200 years (sometimes reaches 1,000 years in the Pacific Northwest)

Habitat: well-drained moist soils, cool shady places

Range: throughout, near cities and parks

Stan's Notes: Very characteristic large cones with distinctive three-point cone scales. Also known as the Coast Douglas-fir or Common Douglas-fir. A very large tree of the Pacific Northwest and Rocky Mountains, where it often grows to over 300 feet (91.5 m) and lives 500 to 1,000 years. Tolerates growing close together in thick stands. Only two of the eight species in the genus *Pseudotsuga* are native to western North America; the other six are native to Asia. *Pseudotsuga* means "false hemlock," referring to its close resemblance to the Eastern Hemlock (pg. 11).

IMMATURE CONE

BARK

CONE

JACK PINE
Pinus banksiana

Family: Pine (Pinaceae)

Height: 20-50' (6-15 m)

Tree: single trunk, many dead branches with very open irregular crown

Needle: clustered needles, 2 per cluster, ¾-1½" (2-4 cm) long, widely forked, each needle is narrow, stiff, slightly twisted, sharply pointed, yellowish green

Bark: reddish gray to black, many loose scales or plates

Cone: yellow green, turning brown to gray at maturity, woody, in pairs, often is curved, 1-2" (2.5-5 cm) long, stalkless, tip pointing down the twig

Origin/Age: native; 100-150 years

Habitat: dry, sandy or rocky soils, poor quality sites, sun

Range: north central and northeastern parts of the state

Stan's Notes: The northernmost pine tree species found in North America and a dominant tree of the Boundary Waters Canoe Area Wilderness, growing on rocky outcroppings and in other dry soils. A very fast-growing tree for the first 20 or so years. Also a pioneer species, being the first conifer to grow after forest fires. Its hard, resinous cones, known as fire cones, can stay closed on the tree for many decades, opening only after exposure to the heat of a fire. The unopened cones are often gathered by squirrels for winter food. Michigan's endangered Kirtland's Warbler is dependent upon Jack Pine, nesting only in young Jack Pine stands after forest fires. The common name "Jack" may refer to its wood, which is used to make levers to jack things up. Also called Gray Pine, Scrub Pine, Banksian Pine or Hudson Bay Pine.

BARK

CONE

PEELING BARK

SCOTCH PINE
Pinus sylvestris

Family: Pine (Pinaceae)

Height: 30-80' (9-24.5 m)

Tree: single trunk that is often crooked, with spreading irregular crown

Needle: clustered needles, 2 per cluster, 1½-3" (4-7.5 cm) long, each needle is stiff, twisted and pointed

Bark: orange brown and flaky lower, bright orange and papery upper

Cone: oval, 1-2½" (2.5-6 cm) long, on a short stalk, in clusters of 2-3, frequently pointing backward up the branch

Origin/Age: non-native, introduced to the U.S. from Europe; 100-150 years

Habitat: well-drained sandy soils, sun

Range: throughout, mostly in the eastern half of the state, along roads, in parks and yards, as shelterbelts

Stan's Notes: One of the more popular Christmas trees grown. Among the first species of trees introduced to North America. The most widely distributed pine in the world, found from Europe to eastern Asia, the Arctic Circle to the Mediterranean Sea, and now North America. In Europe it grows tall and straight, but in North America it seldom has a straight trunk because of the seed source chosen by early settlers; apparently it was easier to collect cones for seeds by climbing trees with crooked trunks. Growing conditions, insect pests and disease also crook trunks. Easily identified by its orange-to-red upper branch bark (see inset) that often peels from the branches in thin papery strips. The main trunk bark has loose scales that fall off to reveal a reddish brown inner bark. Two twisted needles per cluster are characteristic. Also known as Scots Pine.

BARK

CONE

AUSTRIAN PINE
Pinus nigra

Family: Pine (Pinaceae)

Height: 40-60' (12-18 m)

Tree: often irregular-shaped with large, open horizontal branches, broad round crown

Needle: clustered needles, 2 per cluster, 3-6" (7.5-15 cm) long, each needle is twisted, sharply pointed, not breaking cleanly when bent, dark green

Bark: gray brown with reddish branches, very scaly

Cone: green, turning brown at maturity, woody, ovate, 1-3" (2.5-7.5 cm) long, each cone scale ending in a sharp point

Origin/Age: non-native, introduced to the U.S. from southern Europe; 100 or more years

Habitat: wide variety of soils, sun, shade

Range: throughout, mostly in southern half of the state, planted in parks, along roads, as windbreaks and wildlife shelterbelts

Stan's Notes: A very important tree, also known as European Black Pine. Originally from Europe, it was introduced to North America in 1759. This was the first species of trees to be planted during the dedication of the Dust-bowl Shelterbelt Project in 1935. Frequently confused with Red Pine (pg. 23), but easily differentiated from it by the way the needles break. Needles of the Austrian Pine don't break cleanly when bent, like Red Pine needles. Widely planted in parks, and along roads because of its tolerance to salt spray, air pollution and dry soils. Easily grown from seed, it thrives in many soil types and transplants well.

IMMATURE
CONE

BARK

CONE

RED PINE
Pinus resinosa

Family: Pine (Pinaceae)

Height: 40-80' (12-24.5 m)

Tree: single straight trunk, dead lower branches fall off soon after dying, broad round crown

Needle: clustered needles, 2 per cluster, 4-6" (10-15 cm) long, each needle straight, brittle, pointed, breaks when bent, dark green

Bark: reddish brown, becoming redder higher up, many flat scales or plates

Cone: green, turning brown at maturity, 2-3" (5-7.5 cm) long, containing many small brown nutlets

Origin/Age: native; 150-200 years

Habitat: dry sandy soils, often in pure stands, sun

Range: northeastern two-thirds of the state, frequently in mass plantings

Stan's Notes: The official state tree of Minnesota. Very impressive when seen in large pure stands. Often planted for Christmas trees. Also called Norway Pine because early settlers confused the tree with the Norway Spruce of northern Europe. Often confused with Austrian Pine (pg. 21), which has needles as long but which bend without breaking cleanly. Common name comes from its reddish bark. The scaly bark peels off the mature tree and lies at its base, resembling scattered jigsaw puzzle pieces. Branches occur in whorls around the trunk. Cones remain on the tree for several years. Heavy seed crops every four to seven years. Needs a fire to expose mineral soils for seeds to germinate. Used in reforestation projects.

IMMATURE
CONE

BARK

CONE

RESIN

PONDEROSA PINE
Pinus ponderosa

Family: Pine (Pinaceae)

Height: 50-70' (15-21 m)

Tree: single straight trunk, showing little tapering, loses lower branches when mature, irregular crown

Needle: clustered needles, 3 per cluster with occasionally 2 or 5 per cluster on same tree, 5-8" (12.5-20 cm) long, each needle straight, flexible, bending rather than breaking, dark green

Bark: reddish brown with large, long black furrows and some scales

Cone: green, turning brown at maturity, 2-6" (5-15 cm) long, each cone scale armed with a sharp spine

Origin/Age: non-native, introduced to the state from western North America; 150-200 years

Habitat: wide variety of soils, sun

Range: throughout, in parks and yards, as shelterbelts

Stan's Notes: One of the most widely distributed pine tree species in North America and most abundant pine tree in the western U.S. Was also called Western Yellow Pine, but the name was changed in 1932. Also called the Blackjack Pine. It is fast growing, producing a long straight trunk that is prized in the lumber industry for making window sashes, paneling and cabinets. One of the few pine trees that will have three or two (rarely five) needles per cluster. Pieces of fallen bark lay at the base of the tree like jigsaw puzzle pieces. Its thick bark makes the mature tree very fire resistant. Cones contain seeds that are eaten by birds and small animals. Needles and twigs are eaten by deer. Twigs and cones often ooze a clear, fragrant sticky sap resin (see inset) that is often hard to remove from skin or clothing.

BARK

CONE

EASTERN WHITE PINE
Pinus strobus

Family: Pine (Pinaceae)

Height: 70-100' (21-30.5 m)

Tree: single tall trunk, whorls of horizontal branching evenly spaced along trunk with branches concentrating near the top when mature, irregular crown

Needle: clustered needles, 5 per cluster, 3-5" (7.5-12.5 cm) long, each needle is soft, flexible and triangular in cross section

Bark: gray to brown and smooth when young, breaking with age into large broad scales that are separated by deep furrows

Cone: green, turning brown when mature, drooping and curved, 4-8" (10-20 cm) long, pointed white tip on each cone scale, resin-coated

Origin/Age: native; 200-250 years

Habitat: wide variety of soils, from dry and sandy to moist upland sites

Range: north central and northeastern parts of the state, Arrowhead region

Stan's Notes: The largest conifer in Minnesota. A favorite place for Bald Eagles to build their nests. Formerly a dominant tree in the state and the backbone of the timber industry, it was known as the Monarch of the North. Also called Northern White Pine, Soft Pine or Weymouth Pine, the latter name coming from Lord Weymouth, who planted the species on his estate in Wiltshire, England, during the eighteenth century. With many killed by white pine blister rust, a fungus that slowly girdles the trunk, restoration efforts are underway to bring this tree back.

BARK

CONE

TAMARACK
Larix laricina

Family: Pine (Pinaceae)

Height: 40-70' (12-21 m)

Tree: cone shape, single straight trunk, narrow crown

Needle: clustered needles on any twigs and branches older than 1 year, 12-30 per cluster, ¾-1¼" (2-3 cm) long, single needles on current year's growth, each needle is soft, pointed, triangular in cross section, light green

Bark: gray when young, reddish brown and flaky scales with age

Cone: light brown, round, ½-1" (1-2.5 cm) diameter, on a short curved stalk

Fall Color: bright golden yellow

Origin/Age: native; 100-150 years

Habitat: wet soils, swamps, bogs, occasionally in uplands

Range: northern two-thirds of the state

Stan's Notes: A highly unusual species, being the only conifer tree that sheds its leaves each autumn (deciduous). Turns bright golden yellow in the fall before shedding needles. One of the northernmost trees in North America. Often growing with Black Spruce (pg. 5), which also grows in acid bogs and muskegs. Also called Eastern Larch or American Larch. Larch Sawfly larvae eat the needles and in some years can defoliate entire stands of Tamarack. The roots of this tree have been used for lashing wooden slats together.

CONE

BARK

EASTERN REDCEDAR
Juniperus virginiana

Family: Cypress (Cupressaceae)

Height: 25-50' (7.5-15 m)

Tree: pyramid shape, single trunk is frequently crooked or leaning and often fluted with folds and creases, may be divided, with pointed crown

Needle: scaly needles, 1-2" (2.5-5 cm) long, with the scale-like needles overlapping each other, each needle is sharply pointed, round in cross section, dark green

Bark: reddish brown to gray, thin and fibrous, peeling with age into long narrow shreds, reddish inner bark is smooth

Cone: dark blue with a white powdery film, appearing berry-like, ½" (1 cm) long, containing 1-2 seeds

Fall Color: reddish brown during winter

Origin/Age: native; 300 years

Habitat: dry soils, open hillsides, wet swampy areas, sun

Range: throughout

Stan's Notes: One of the first trees to grow back in fields or prairies after a fire. Often seen covering hillsides. Slow growing, producing what appear to be blue berries, which are actually cones. Cones are used to flavor gin during the distillation process. Many bird species spread seeds by eating cones, dispersing seeds in their droppings. Redcedar wood is aromatic, lightweight and used in many ways. Often used to make storage chests, lending its pleasant smell to blankets and other linen. The smooth reddish inner bark was called baton rouge or red stick by early French settlers who found the tree growing in Louisiana. Affected by cedar-apple rust, which causes large jelly-like orange growths. Its sharply pointed leaves can cause slight skin irritation. Also called Eastern Juniper or Red Juniper.

IMMATURE
CONE

MATURE
CONE

BARK

EASTERN WHITE-CEDAR
Thuja occidentalis

Family: Cypress (Cupressaceae)

Height: 30-50' (9-15 m)

Tree: pyramid shape, single or multiple trunks are often crooked or twisted, blunt or pointed dense crown

Needle: scaly needles, 1-2" (2.5-5 cm) long, with the scale-like needles overlapping each other and forming flat evergreen leaves, each needle soft, flat in cross section, light green

Bark: gray and fibrous with shallow furrows, peeling in long strips

Cone: green, turning light brown at maturity, ½" (1 cm) long, upright in clusters, containing 2 tiny winged nutlets (seeds)

Origin/Age: native; 150-200 years (some reach 800 years)

Habitat: moist or wet soils, often in pure stands

Range: northeastern quarter of the state

Stan's Notes: A common tree of bogs and swamps, and favorite food of deer during winter. Slow growing but a very long life, with some trees over 700 years old. The green cones turn brown when they are mature and ready to release seeds. Also known as Northern White-Cedar, Eastern Thuja or Eastern Arborvitae. The common name "Arborvitae," meaning "tree of life," may have come from French voyagers who used the white-cedar to treat scurvy, a disease resulting from a lack of vitamin C. The lightweight wood was once used for canoe frames. One of only two species of *Thuja* in North America, it was introduced into Europe by the mid-1500s. More than 100 different varieties are known for this tree.

THORN

BARK

FLOWER

FRUIT

EUROPEAN BUCKTHORN
Rhamnus cathartica

Family: Buckthorn (Rhamnaceae)

Height: 10-20' (3-6 m)

Tree: single to multiple crooked trunks, round crown

Leaf: simple, oval, 1-3" (2.5-7.5 cm) length, oppositely attached, pointed tip, fine-toothed margin, curved and slightly sunken veins, dark green above

Bark: gray, many horizontal white marks (lenticels) and many scales, tiny spine (thorn) in the forkings at ends of twigs

Flower: green bell-shaped flower, ¼" (.6 cm) in diameter, in clusters

Fruit: green berry, turning black at maturity, ¼" (.6 cm) in diameter, in clusters, containing 3-4 seeds and remaining on tree throughout winter

Fall Color: green, remaining on tree long after leaves of other trees have dropped

Origin/Age: non-native, introduced from Europe; 25-50 years

Habitat: wide variety of soils

Range: throughout

Stan's Notes: About 100 species of buckthorn trees and shrubs, 12 native to North America. One of two European species that escaped from landscaping. Now naturalized throughout Minnesota. Grows in thick stands, shading out native plants, making it undesirable. Considered a nuisance, many state and city agencies have programs to eliminate it from parks and woodland. Leaves stay green well into November before falling. Spread by birds, which eat the berries in large quantities in winter. One of the few berries available for birds returning in spring. Berries are cathartic (cause diarrhea) and can cause severe dehydration. Also called Common Buckthorn.

BARK

FLOWER

FRUIT

EASTERN WAHOO
Euonymus atropurpureus

Family: Staff-tree (Celastraceae)

Height: 20-25' (6-7.5 m)

Tree: single or multiple trunks, irregular crown

Leaf: simple, oval, 2-5" (5-12.5 cm) length, oppositely attached, pointed tip, fine-toothed margin, dull green with hairy undersides

Bark: greenish gray with reddish brown streaks, smooth

Flower: 4-parted purple flower

Fruit: 4-lobed capsule, turning pink to red at maturity, ½" (1 cm) long, containing 4 seeds

Fall Color: red

Origin/Age: native; 25-50 years

Habitat: moist soils, usually is found along streams, rivers and floodplains

Range: southeastern quarter of the state

Stan's Notes: Also known as the Spindle Tree or Burning-bush Euonymus, it's the only *Euonymus* tree species native to Minnesota. The pinkish capsules each contain four seeds, which have a fleshy covering. Capsules stay on tree into winter, with the fleshy fruit and seeds providing a good source of food for birds. Spread by birds. Twigs have distinctive corky ridges or wings. Over 150 species in the world, nearly all in Asia, with one tree and four shrub species in North America. Several of the shrubby *Euonymus* species that were introduced are also called Burning-bush.

FRUIT

BARK

FLOWER

LEAFSTALK

NANNYBERRY
Viburnum lentago

Family: Honeysuckle (Caprifoliaceae)

Height: 10-20' (3-6 m)

Tree: appearing like a large shrub with multi-stemmed trunk, drooping branches and dense round crown

Leaf: simple, oval, 3-5" (7.5-12.5 cm) long, oppositely attached, pointed tip, fine-toothed margin, shiny green, leafstalk (petiole) is flattened to U-shaped with many swellings (glands)

Bark: gray and smooth, many horizontal lines (lenticels), sometimes with small scales

Flower: white flower, ¼" (.6 cm) wide, in flat clusters, 3-5" (7.5-12.5 cm) wide

Fruit: green berry-like fruit, turning dark purple when mature, appearing like a raisin, sweet and edible, round, ¼-½" (.6-1 cm) diameter, in clusters, has 1 seed

Fall Color: red to reddish purple

Origin/Age: native; 10-20 years

Habitat: wide variety of soils from wet to dry, along forest edges, on stream banks and hillsides

Range: throughout

Stan's Notes: Over 100 species in the world with over 20 native to North America. Also known as Blackhaw, Sweet Viburnum or Wild Raisin, the latter name referring to the taste and texture of the fruit when ripe in late summer. Although the fruit is sweet and edible, the large seed within makes it hard to eat. A favorite food of wildlife when ripe. Grooved or winged leafstalk (see inset) helps to identify the tree. Often along edges of forest, swamps, marshes and streams.

39

FLOWER

BARK

FRUIT

NORTHERN CATALPA
Catalpa speciosa

Family:	Trumpet-Creeper (Bignoniaceae)
Height:	50-75' (15-23 m)
Tree:	single trunk, large round crown
Leaf:	simple, heart-shaped, 6-12" (15-30 cm) in length, oppositely attached or whorls of 3 leaves, margin lacking teeth, dull green
Bark:	light brown with deep furrows, flat-topped ridges
Flower:	large, showy orchid-like flower is cream to white with yellow and purple spots and stripes, 2-3" (5-7.5 cm) long, in clusters, 5-8" (12.5-20 cm) wide, fragrant odor
Fruit:	long bean-like green capsule, turning to brown at maturity, 8-18" (20-45 cm) long, splitting open into 2 parts, containing winged seeds
Fall Color:	yellow green, turning black
Origin/Age:	non-native, was introduced to the state from the central Mississippi Valley; 40-50 years
Habitat:	rich moist soils
Range:	isolated in cities and parks throughout southern two-thirds of the state, old home sites

Stan's Notes: Catalpa tree leaves are among the largest leaves in the state. About a dozen catalpa species, two native to North America. This is a non-native tree that has been successfully planted along streets and boulevards in just about every city in the southern two-thirds of Minnesota. Its name "Catalpa" is an American Indian name for this tree, but it is also called Catawba, Cigar Tree or Indian Bean, which all refer to the large seedpods (fruit). Its large showy flowers bloom in spring and attract many insects. Twigs have a soft white pith.

FRUIT

BARK

SIBERIAN ELM
Ulmus pumila

Family: Elm (Ulmaceae)

Height: 30-50' (9-15 m)

Tree: single trunk, open irregular crown

Leaf: simple, narrow, ¾-2" (2-5 cm) length, alternately attached, with pointed tip, asymmetrical leaf base, double-toothed margin, dark green

Bark: gray with rough scales

Fruit: flat green disk (samara), lacking hair when young, turning papery brown when mature, ½" (1 cm) diameter, with a closed notch opposite fruit stalk

Fall Color: yellow

Origin/Age: non-native, introduced from Asia; 50-75 years

Habitat: wide variety of soils

Range: throughout, in parks, hedges, old home sites

Stan's Notes: A small non-native species that was introduced from Asia, with some of the smallest leaves of any of the elm trees. Fast growing, but doesn't attain the height or reach the age of American Elm (pg. 47). The species name means "small," referring to the tree's small stature. Also called Chinese Elm. Chinese Elm (*U. parvifolia*), however, is a cultivated species and is not the same. Naturalized in the Great Plains from Minnesota south to Kansas and west to Utah. Will thrive in a wide variety of soils and tolerate harsh conditions. Resistant to Dutch elm disease.

BARK

ROCK ELM
Ulmus thomasii

Family: Elm (Ulmaceae)

Height: 40-60' (12-18 m)

Tree: medium-sized tree with single straight trunk and drooping branches, tall narrow crown

Leaf: simple, oval, 2-4" (5-10 cm) in length, alternately attached, asymmetrical leaf base, double-toothed margin, deep green above and slightly paler green below, finely hairy

Bark: dark gray, tinged with red, alternating layers of white and brown when seen in cross section, scaly with broad flat-topped ridges

Flower: green flower, ⅛" (.3 cm) wide, hanging in clusters, 1-1½" (2.5-4 cm) wide, on slender stalks, appears before leaves each spring

Fruit: thin green disk (samara), turning to brown when mature, round to oval, ¼-¾" (.6-2 cm) diameter, with a shallowly notched tip that is opposite the fruit stalk, covered with fine white hairs

Fall Color: yellow

Origin/Age: native; 175 years

Habitat: dry soils, heavy clay, rocky cliffs, full sun

Range: scattered throughout the southern half of the state

Stan's Notes: The hardest, heaviest and strongest, but least elm-like of native elms. It can be quickly identified by the irregular corky bark on young twigs and branches. Also called Cork Elm because of the corky bark on twigs. Main trunk is distinct almost to the top. Not a common tree throughout. Common name "Rock" may come from its habit of growing on rocky ridges and bluffs. Wood was used to make pianos, but is rarely used for that purpose now.

BARK

FLOWER

FRUIT

AMERICAN ELM
Ulmus americana

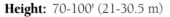

Family: Elm (Ulmaceae)

Height: 70-100' (21-30.5 m)

Tree: one of the tallest of trees, single trunk, prominent root flares, upper limbs fan out gracefully, forming an upright vase shape, branch tips often drooping

Leaf: simple, oval, 3-6" (7.5-15 cm) length, alternately attached, with pointed tip, asymmetrical leaf base, double-toothed margin, slightly rough to touch, only 2-3 forked veins per leaf

Bark: dark gray, deeply furrowed with flat ridges, corky, sometimes scaly

Flower: tiny reddish brown flower, ¼" (.6 cm) diameter, in clusters, 1" (2.5 cm) wide

Fruit: flat, fuzzy green disk (samara), turning tan when mature, round to oval, ½" (1 cm) diameter, with a notch opposite the fruit stalk

Fall Color: yellow

Origin/Age: native; 150-200 years

Habitat: moist soils, full sun

Range: throughout

Stan's Notes: Also called White Elm, this once dominant tree lined just about every city street in eastern North America. Nearly eliminated due to Dutch elm disease, which is caused by a fungus that attacks the tree's vascular system. The fungus was introduced to the U.S. in the 1920s by infected elm logs from Europe. Its arching branches form a canopy, providing shade. The distinct vase shape of the mature tree makes it easy to recognize from a distance.

BARK

FRUIT

SLIPPERY ELM
Ulmus rubra

Family: Elm (Ulmaceae)

Height: 50-70' (15-21 m)

Tree: single trunk is divided high, ascending branches, broad flat-topped crown

Leaf: simple, oval, 4-7" (10-18 cm) length, alternately attached, widest above the middle, asymmetrical leaf base, approximately 26-30 veins with some forked near margin, rough and dark green above, paler below, short leafstalk

Bark: brown to reddish brown, shallow furrows, vertical irregular flat scales, inner bark reddish

Fruit: green disk (samara), turning brown when mature, nearly round, ½-¾" (1-2 cm) in diameter, with a slightly notched tip opposite the fruit stalk, few reddish brown hairs

Fall Color: yellow

Origin/Age: native; 100-125 years

Habitat: rich moist soils, along streams, slopes

Range: southern half of the state

Stan's Notes: Due to its habit of growing near water, sometimes is called Water Elm. More often called Red Elm because of its reddish inner bark. The inner bark is fragrant and mucilaginous, hence its common name, Slippery. Scientific name was formerly *U. fulva*. The inner bark was once chewed to quench thirst and used to cure sore throats. Leaves are smaller than those of most other elm species and very rough to touch. Look for some forked veins near the margin. Leaf buds are dark rusty brown and covered with hairs, making this tree easy to identify even without its leaves.

BARK

FLOWER

FRUIT

QUAKING ASPEN
Populus tremuloides

Family: Willow (Salicaceae)

Height: 40-70' (12-21 m)

Tree: slender tree, straight trunk, lacking any major side branches, round crown

Leaf: simple, nearly round, 1-3" (2.5-7.5 cm) in length, alternately attached, with short sharp point, fine-toothed margin, shiny green above and dull green below, leafstalk (petiole) flattened

Bark: dark gray to brown in color and deeply furrowed lower, greenish white to cream and smooth upper

Flower: catkin, 1-2" (2.5-5 cm) in length, male and female bloom (flower) on separate trees in spring before the leaves bud

Fruit: catkin-like fruit, 4" (10 cm) long, is composed of many tiny green capsules, ⅛" (.3 cm) long, that open and release seeds, seeds attached to white cottony material and float on the wind

Fall Color: golden yellow

Origin/Age: native; 60-80 years

Habitat: wet or dry, sandy or rocky soils

Range: throughout

Stan's Notes: The most widely distributed tree in Minnesota and North America. Name refers to the leaves, which catch very gentle breezes and shake or quake in wind. Also called Trembling Aspen or Popple. Grows in large, often pure stands. Returns from its own roots if cut or toppled. Most reproduce by suckering off their roots, which creates clone trees. One stand in Utah–106 acres (42 ha) in size with about 47,000 trunks–is the largest single living organism in the world. Has survived lab temperatures of -314°F (-192°C).

BARK

FRUIT

BIGTOOTH ASPEN
Populus grandidentata

Family: Willow (Salicaceae)

Height: 50-70' (15-21 m)

Tree: single trunk with few lower branches and a round irregular crown

Leaf: simple, oval to triangular, 3-6" (7.5-15 cm) long, alternately attached, blunt tip, frequently with 30-34 large saw-like blunt teeth, waxy above, has a long flattened leafstalk

Bark: gray in color with deep furrows and thick ridges lower, pale green to white and smooth upper

Flower: catkin, 4-5" (10-12.5 cm) long

Fruit: catkin-like fruit, 4" (10 cm) long, is composed of many tiny narrow capsules, ⅛" (.3 cm) long, that split open into 2 parts and release cottony seeds

Fall Color: yellow

Origin/Age: native; 50-75 years

Habitat: moist soils

Range: eastern two-thirds of the state

Stan's Notes: One of over 40 species of poplar found throughout the northern hemisphere. A fast-growing, short-lived tree. Woolly hairs cover leaves in spring, but by summer they will have turned thick and waxy. Also called Largetooth Aspen, as each leaf often has 30 to 34 large teeth. The leafstalk (petiole) is flattened and often as long as the leaf. Its large leaves catch the slightest breezes, causing rustling in the same way as the Quaking Aspen (pg. 51). Male and female flowers grow on separate trees. Produces heavy seed crops every three to five years.

BARK

LOMBARDY POPLAR
Populus nigra

Family: Willow (Salicaceae)

Height: 60-80' (18-24 m)

Tree: single straight trunk, ascending branches, narrow columnar crown

Leaf: simple, triangular, 2-4" (5-10 cm) long, alternately attached, often wider than long, pointed tip, fine-toothed margin, dark green above, paler below

Bark: gray with deep furrows lower and smooth upper

Fruit: capsule, ¼" (.6 cm) long, containing many seeds

Fall Color: yellow to brown

Origin/Age: non-native, introduced from Italy; 30-50 years

Habitat: wide variety of soils, sun

Range: throughout, planted in windrows, an ornamental in yards and parks

Stan's Notes: A uniquely tall thin tree, usually seen in cities, parks or near older homesteads. Unable to reproduce because all trees planted are males. Often planted in a single row, it was once planted much more than it is planted now. Removed from many city parks because of its non-native status. Fast growing, but short-lived due to its susceptibility to various canker diseases. The species name *nigra* refers to its dark patchy bark. The common name "Lombardy" is also the name of a region in Italy. Known for lining the streets of many Italian cities. Also known as Black Poplar.

UNDERSIDE

BARK

FRUIT

BALSAM POPLAR
Populus balsamifera

Family: Willow (Salicaceae)

Height: 50-70' (15-21 m)

Tree: single trunk with ascending branches and narrow open crown

Leaf: simple, triangular, 3-6" (7.5-15 cm) length, alternately attached, fine-toothed margin, shiny green above, silvery green below with resinous, fragrant rust-colored blotches, round leafstalk

Bark: greenish brown color when young, aging to gray, smooth with many cracks and fissures

Flower: catkin, 3-4" (7.5-10 cm) long

Fruit: catkin-like fruit, 3-4" (7.5-10 cm) long, composed of many tiny capsules, ⅛" (.3 cm) long, that split open into 2 parts and release seeds, seeds attached to cottony hair and float on the wind

Fall Color: yellow

Origin/Age: native; 50-75 years

Habitat: moist soils, river valleys, shade intolerant

Range: northern half of the state

Stan's Notes: It's easy to smell this tree–simply walk nearby it. Small branches pruned during springtime can be brought inside for a wonderful spicy fragrance. In the spring, its leaf buds are covered with a sticky, fragrant resin. Later, the rust-colored resin covers the undersides of leaves. Fast growing, shade intolerant, often growing in pure stands or mixed with aspens. Its species name is Latin and refers to the odor. Also known as Balm-of-Gilead, which refers to the alleged medicinal properties of the resin.

BARK

SEEDS

EASTERN COTTONWOOD
Populus deltoides

Family: Willow (Salicaceae)

Height: 70-100' (21-30.5 m)

Tree: large tree with single or multiple trunks, few lower branches and huge, broad irregular crown

Leaf: simple, triangular, 3-6" (7.5-15 cm) length, alternately attached, coarse-toothed margin, thick and waxy, shiny green above and below, leafstalk long and flattened

Bark: gray with deep flat furrows

Flower: catkin, 2-3" (5-7.5 cm) long

Fruit: catkin-like fruit, 4" (10 cm) long, is composed of many tiny capsules, ¼" (.6 cm) long, that split open into 4 parts and release seeds, seeds attached to cottony hair and float on the wind

Fall Color: yellow

Origin/Age: native; 50-200 years

Habitat: wet soils, along streams, rivers and lakes

Range: throughout, except for the northeastern quarter of the state, planted in wet areas

Stan's Notes: A huge tree of riverbanks (floodplains) and other wet areas. Some trees can obtain heights of 150 feet (46 m), with trunk diameters of 7 to 8 feet (2.1 to 2.4 m). Fast growing, up to 5 feet (1.5 m) in height and over 1 inch (2.5 cm) in diameter per year. Like many others in its genus, the leafstalks are flat. Species name *deltoides* is Latin, describing the delta-shaped leaf. Known for the massive release of seed-bearing "cotton," hence its common name.

BARK

FRUIT

RIVER BIRCH
Betula nigra

SIMPLE
ALTERNATE

Family: Birch (Betulaceae)

Height: 40-60' (12-18 m)

Tree: medium-sized tree, single or multiple trunks and spreading irregular crown

Leaf: simple, oval, 2-3" (5-7.5 cm) in length, alternately attached, sometimes with asymmetrical leaf base, double-toothed margin, dark green above, paler green below

Bark: reddish brown to salmon pink, some shaggy curly bark, often flaky, becoming dark and scaly with age

Fruit: many winged nutlets, each ⅛" (.3 cm) wide, in a cone-like seed catkin, 1" (2.5 cm) long

Fall Color: yellow

Origin/Age: native; 50-75 years

Habitat: wet soils, in river valleys, along streams, wetlands and lakes, shade tolerant

Range: along the Minnesota and Mississippi Rivers in the southeastern quarter, and in several other major river valleys

Stan's Notes: This is the southernmost birch tree species in North America, growing as far south as Florida and Texas, and the only birch to disperse its seeds in spring. "River" refers to its habitat near water, where it plays a major role in erosion control. "Birch" comes from the Old German *birka*, meaning "bright," presumably referring to its light bark. Leaves tend to be smaller than Yellow Birch (pg. 67). Trunk can grow to 1 to 1½ feet (30-45 cm) wide; often covered with a salmon pink curled bark. Widely planted as a landscape tree, it is the only native birch resistant to Bronze Birch Borer beetle larvae, which tunnel through inner bark, causing branches or the entire tree to die. Wood is rarely used for any commercial application.

61

BARK

SWEET BIRCH
Betula lenta

Family: Birch (Betulaceae)

Height: 50-70' (15-21 m)

Tree: single straight trunk, round irregular crown

Leaf: simple, oval, 2-3" (5-7.5 cm) in length, alternately attached, with a pointed tip, fine-toothed margin and straight veins with only a few forked near the margin, yellowish green above, lighter below

Bark: brownish red and smooth when young, turning darker with furrows, often becoming scaly

Fruit: many winged nutlets, each ⅛" (.3 cm) wide, in a cone-like seed catkin, ½-1" (1-2.5 cm) long, that grows upright on branch

Fall Color: yellow

Origin/Age: non-native, introduced from eastern states; 100-150 years

Habitat: rich moist soils

Range: southern half of the state

Stan's Notes: Also called Cherry Birch or Black Birch, both names referring to the color of the bark, which is red and smooth when young but turns dark with age. Fresh twigs that are broken or crushed release a strong scent of wintergreen (methyl salicylate). Very similar to the Yellow Birch (pg. 67), the only major differences being hairy leaf buds, and reddish brown bark when older. Can be tapped for sap, which when boiled down makes a syrup. European settlers made birch beer from the syrup and honey, then fermenting it. Resistant to Bronze Birch Borers, which kill most birch species.

FRUIT

BARK

PAPER BIRCH
Betula papyrifera

Family: Birch (Betulaceae)

Height: 40-60' (12-18 m)

Tree: single or multiple crooked trunks with drooping branches and open narrow crown

Leaf: simple, oval to triangular, 2-4" (5-10 cm) length, alternately attached, pointed tip, double-toothed margin, 18 or fewer veins, each ending in a large tooth, dull green above, paler below

Bark: white and smooth with obvious dark horizontal lines (lenticels), often shedding in curled sheets, inner bark reddish

Flower: catkin, 1-2" (2.5-5 cm) long

Fruit: many winged nutlets, each ⅛" (.3 cm) wide, in a cone-like seed catkin, 1-2" (2.5-5 cm) long

Fall Color: yellow

Origin/Age: native; 80-100 years

Habitat: moist soils

Range: northeastern two-thirds of the state, planted in cities and parks

Stan's Notes: Also called White Birch or Canoe Birch, both names referring to the white bark that American Indians used to construct canoes, baskets and water containers. Dried bark often used to start campfires. Understory tree that likes moist soil and high humidity. Often doesn't grow well when planted by itself in a sunny suburban lawn. When stressed, trees are attacked by destructive Bronze Birch Borers. Both male and female flowers are on the same tree. Winged nutlets released from seed catkins in early winter cover snow under the tree. Found across the northern portion of North America.

BARK

FRUIT

YELLOW BIRCH
Betula alleghaniensis

Family: Birch (Betulaceae)

Height: 50-70' (15-21 m)

Tree: single trunk with spreading branches and tips that droop, round irregular crown

Leaf: simple, oval to lance-shaped, 3-5" (7.5-12.5 cm) length, alternately attached, pointed tip, double-toothed margin, dull green

Bark: bronze to yellow in color, thin horizontal marks (lenticels), covered with thin papery scales often curling up in rolls

Flower: catkin, 1-2" (2.5-5 cm) long

Fruit: many winged nutlets, ⅛" (.3 cm) wide, contained in a cone-like seed catkin, 1" (2.5 cm) long, that grows upright on branch

Fall Color: yellow

Origin/Age: native; 100-125 years

Habitat: rich moist soils, often in wet places

Range: northern half of the state

Stan's Notes: One of the tallest of the birches, often thought to be underutilized in landscaping. Also called Swamp Birch due to its nature of growing in wet areas. Species name *alleghaniensis* means "yellow" and refers to its bronze-to-yellow bark. The bark is very characteristic, making this species one of easier birches to identify. Twigs are aromatic of wintergreen (methyl salicylate) when crushed. A pleasant-tasting tea can be made from the tender twigs. Wood is used to make furniture and veneers. Will produce heavy seed crops every couple years. Seedlings are heavily browsed by deer.

FRUIT

BARK

FLOWER

CRAB APPLE
Malus spp.

Family: Rose (Rosaceae)

Height: 10-20' (3-6 m)

Tree: single crooked trunk, open broad crown

Leaf: simple, oval, 2-3" (5-7.5 cm) in length, alternately attached, sometimes with shallow lobes, double-toothed margin, dark green above, lighter-colored and usually smooth or hairless below

Bark: gray, many scales, with 1-2" (2.5-5 cm) long stout thorns often on twigs

Flower: 5-petaled white-to-pink or red flower that is often very showy, 1-2" (2.5-5 cm) wide

Fruit: apple, ranging in color from green and yellow to red, edible, 1-3" (2.5-7.5 cm) diameter, single or in small clusters, hanging from a long fruit stalk well into winter

Fall Color: yellow to red

Origin/Age: non-native, escaped from yards or old farm homesteads; 25-50 years

Habitat: wide variety of soils, sun

Range: throughout, often around cities or old home sites

Stan's Notes: Many species of cultivated Crab Apple can be found throughout the state with only one, Prairie Crab Apple (*M. ioensis*), native to southeastern Minnesota. Others have escaped cultivation and now grow in the wild. Introduced to the U.S. in colonial times. Now found throughout the country. Apples are closely related to those sold in grocery stores, and have been used in jams and jellies. Cider is often made from the more tart apples. Fruit is an important food source for wildlife. Twigs often have long stout thorns, which are actually modified branches known as spur branches.

BARK

FLOWER

FRUIT

WILD APPLE
Malus spp.

Family: Rose (Rosaceae)

Height: 10-15' (3-4.5 m)

Tree: single crooked trunk, many spreading branches, creating a broad round crown

Leaf: simple, oval, 2-4" (5-10 cm) length, blunt-tipped, fine-toothed margin, dark green in color, densely hairy below

Bark: brown, scaly with peeling edges

Flower: 5-petaled showy white (sometimes streaked with pink) flower, 1-2" (2.5-5 cm) wide

Fruit: apple, edible with typical shape and size, 2-4" (5-10 cm) diameter

Fall Color: brown

Origin/Age: non-native; 25-50 years

Habitat: dry soils, along fencerows and roadsides, sun

Range: throughout

Stan's Notes: A direct descendent from the ancestors of cultivated apples now sold in grocery stores. Introduced in colonial times to the U.S. along with the Crab Apple (pg. 69). Found throughout the country now. The apples are edible and some are very delicious. The fruit has been used in jellies and desserts such as pies. These trees, usually associated with former homesteads, are found along roads or fencerows where seedlings were planted or where apples were discarded and seeds have taken root. Wide varieties of Wild Apple species are now naturalized in Minnesota.

UNDERSIDE

BARK

FLOWER

FRUIT

JUNEBERRY
Amelanchier arborea

Family: Rose (Rosaceae)

Height: 10-20' (3-6 m)

Tree: multiple narrow trunks, round crown

Leaf: simple, oval, 2-4" (5-10 cm) in length, alternately attached, pointed tip, fine-toothed margin (sometimes toothless near stalk), dark green above, whitish hairs below (see inset) and covering stalk

Bark: light gray, smooth with shallow cracks

Flower: erect white flower, 1" (2.5 cm) long, in clusters, 1-3" (2.5-7.5 cm) wide

Fruit: red fruit, turning dark blue when mature, edible, round, ¼" (.6 cm) diameter, on a fruit stalk, in hanging clusters

Fall Color: yellow to red

Origin/Age: native; 10-20 years

Habitat: dry soils, hillsides, forest edges, open fields, sun

Range: throughout

Stan's Notes: There are 16 species of *Amelanchier* in the world, most occurring in North America. In Minnesota we have several varieties of Juneberry, but they are difficult to differentiate because of crossbreeding among species. Called Juneberry because the fruit ripens in June. Fruit is edible and an important food source for wildlife. Also called Downy Serviceberry, with the name "Downy" for the whitish downy hairs on undersides of leaves (see inset) and covering the leafstalks, and "Serviceberry" because it flowers during spring coincidentally with cemetery burials of northern climates. It is also known as Shadbush because the blooming time occurs when shad fishes spawn.

BARK

FRUIT

ROUNDLEAF SERVICEBERRY
Amelanchier sanguinea

Family: Rose (Rosaceae)

Height: 10-20' (3-6 m)

Tree: multiple narrow round trunks

Leaf: simple, round to oval, 2-4" (5-10 cm) long, alternately attached, leaf tip often rounded or blunt, coarse-toothed margin, dark green

Bark: light gray in color, smooth texture with narrow whitish vertical ridges

Flower: white flower, ½-1" (1-2.5 cm) wide, in drooping clusters, 1-4" (2.5-10 cm) long

Fruit: bright red berry, turning dark purple at maturity, edible when ripe, ¼-½" (.6-1 cm) diameter, on a ½-1" (1-2.5 cm) long fruit stalk

Fall Color: yellow to red

Origin/Age: native; 25-50 years

Habitat: wide variety of soils, hillsides, forest edges, open fields, sun

Range: throughout

Stan's Notes: One of several species of serviceberry in Minnesota. It often crossbreeds with other serviceberrys, making it one of the harder tree species to identify. Leaves each have up to 40 teeth, and are densely hairy when unfolding early in spring. Flowering occurs when leaves start to unfurl. Twigs often are red to reddish brown. Ripe fruit, which is dark purple, juicy and edible, is an important food for wildlife. Fruit is used as an ingredient for jams and jellies, and is also fermented into an intoxicating drink.

UNDERSIDE

BARK

FLOWER

WEEPING WILLOW
Salix babylonica

Family: Willow (Salicaceae)

Height: 40-80' (12-24.5 m)

Tree: single trunk, often crooked, with many drooping branches often reaching the ground, very broad round crown

Leaf: simple, narrow lance-shaped, 2-4" (5-10 cm) long, alternately attached, pointed tip and fine-toothed margin, bright green above, whitish below

Bark: light brown with many medium furrows and flat-topped corky ridges

Flower: catkin, 1" (2.5 cm) long, standing erect on a short leafy shoot

Fruit: catkin-like fruit, 1" (2.5 cm) long, is composed of many small capsules that open and release seeds, seeds attached to white cottony material

Fall Color: yellow

Origin/Age: non-native, introduced from Asia; 75-100 years

Habitat: wet or moist soils

Range: throughout, an ornamental in yards and parks

Stan's Notes: Also known as Golden Willow because of its yellow twigs and fall color. The twigs are very flexible and hang nearly to the ground. Many branches break off in heavy winds. Often seen growing along the shores of ponds and lakes. Not as commonly planted anymore. An extract from willow bark (salicin) was used as an early form of aspirin. Also called Babylon Weeping Willow.

FRUIT

BARK

LAUREL WILLOW
Salix pentandra

Family: Willow (Salicaceae)

Height: 25-45' (7.5-14 m)

Tree: appearing like a large shrub with multi-stemmed trunk, round irregular crown

Leaf: simple, lance-shaped, 2-5" (5-12.5 cm) in length, alternately attached, pointed tip and fine-toothed margin, distinct yellow midrib, pleasant fragrance when crushed, very shiny dark green above, dull green below

Bark: gray, smooth when young, cracking with age into flat irregular ridges

Flower: golden yellow catkin, 1-2" (2.5-5 cm) long, on a short stalk

Fruit: catkin-like fruit, 1-2" (2.5-5 cm) long, composed of many capsules, ¼" (.6 cm) long, seeds within

Fall Color: yellow

Origin/Age: non-native, introduced from Europe and western Asia; 20-40 years

Habitat: wet acid soils

Range: throughout, isolated in and around cities, parks

Stan's Notes: A fast-growing and short-lived tree also known as Bay-leaved Willow. Although a non-native tree, it is one of the most widespread and successful of the many willow species in Minnesota, each difficult to identify. Has one of the wider leaves of the willow species. Leaves have been used for flavoring foods and often remain on tree into autumn. Has been planted in yards, parks and along roads in shelterbelts because it is a relatively disease-free species. Thrives well north into Canada.

FRUIT

BARK

FLOWER

PUSSY WILLOW
Salix discolor

Family: Willow (Salicaceae)

Height: 10-20' (3-6 m)

Tree: small tree, multiple trunks, irregular crown

Leaf: simple, lance-shaped, 2-5" (5-12.5 cm) in length, alternately attached, with shallow irregular teeth, smooth to touch, shiny green above, paler below, lacking hairs, young leaves often reddish and very hairy, 2 small appendages (stipules) on leafstalk

Bark: gray to brown, often red tinges, shallow furrows

Flower: catkin, ½-1" (1-2.5 cm) long, covered with silky hairs when immature, lacking a stalk

Fruit: catkin-like fruit, ½-1" (1-2.5 cm) long, composed of many capsules, ¼" (.6 cm) long, seeds within

Fall Color: yellow

Origin/Age: native; 20-50 years

Habitat: wet soils, along shores, swamps, wetlands

Range: throughout, except for the extreme southwestern quarter of the state

Stan's Notes: Likely the most common and widespread willow in Minnesota, certainly the best known. The immature catkins, which are covered with silky hairs known as pussy fur, are often collected and used in floral arrangements early in spring. Twigs are reddish purple with orange dots (lenticels). The species name *discolor* refers to the pale undersides of the leaves. Look for tiny leaf-like stipules on the leafstalk, and the contrasting green upper and whitish lower leaf surfaces to help identify.

BARK

FRUIT

BLACK WILLOW
Salix nigra

Family: Willow (Salicaceae)

Height: 40-60' (12-18 m)

Tree: single crooked trunk, often forked, with a narrow irregular crown

Leaf: simple, narrow lance-shaped, 3-6" (7.5-15 cm) in length, alternately attached, fine-toothed margin, shiny green above and below, short leafstalk often has tiny leaf-like appendages (stipules), making the leaf appear to be clasping the twig

Bark: dark brown color and deeply furrowed into large patchy scales with flat-topped ridges

Flower: catkin, 2-3" (5-7.5 cm) long, hanging down

Fruit: catkin-like fruit, 2-3" (5-7.5 cm) long, composed of many capsules, ¼" (.6 cm) long, seeds within

Fall Color: light yellow

Origin/Age: native; 50-75 years

Habitat: wet soils, stream banks, wetlands and other wet places, shade intolerant

Range: southeastern quarter of the state

Stan's Notes: The largest of our native willows in Minnesota. Its common name comes from the dark bark. Fast-growing, but a short-lived tree that doesn't tolerate shade. Also known as Swamp Willow, it is commonly found along streams, rivers and other wet places. Often hybridizes with Crack Willow (*S. fragilis*), a species more common in southern states. Twigs are light yellow to reddish, downy when young, becoming gray and hairless. Branches are spreading and easily broken by high winds. Look for the large leaves and leaf-like stipules to help identify.

FRUIT

BARK

RED MULBERRY
Morus rubra

Family: Mulberry (Moraceae)

Height: 20-30' (6-9 m)

Tree: single trunk, divided low, with spreading branches and dense round crown

Leaf: simple, oval to multi-lobed, 2-5" (5-12.5 cm) in length, alternately attached, with coarse-toothed margin, exudes milky sap when torn, shiny green above, hairy tufts below

Bark: gray to reddish brown with uneven furrows

Fruit: green berry (aggregate fruit), turning red to black, appearing like a raspberry, made up of many tiny 1-seeded fruit, sweet and edible, ½" (1 cm) wide

Fall Color: yellow

Origin/Age: native; 50-75 years

Habitat: moist soils, floodplains, river valleys

Range: southeastern quarter of the state

Stan's Notes: One of two mulberry tree species in Minnesota, the second being White Mulberry (pg. 87), an introduced species. It produces large crops of fruit, providing an important food source for wildlife, especially birds. In summer, berries ripen to red and are delicious when black. Fruit is sweet and juicy, used in jams, jellies and pies. New trees are started when seeds pass through digestive tracts of birds unharmed and are deposited. Its common name and the species name *rubra* refer to its mostly red fruit. Early settlers and American Indians used its fresh fruit to make beverages, cakes and preserves, and medicinally to cure dysentery and other ailments.

BARK

FRUIT

WHITE MULBERRY
Morus alba

Family: Mulberry (Moraceae)

Height: 10-30' (3-9 m)

Tree: small tree, single trunk is often divided low, open round crown

Leaf: simple, oval to multi-lobed, 2-5" (5-12.5 cm) in length, alternately attached, with coarse-toothed margin, exudes milky sap when torn, shiny green above, hairy tufts below

Bark: orange brown, deeply furrowed with flat ridges

Fruit: pink, purple or white berry (aggregate fruit) with a raspberry-like appearance, made of many tiny 1-seeded fruit, sweet and edible, ½" (1 cm) wide

Fall Color: yellow

Origin/Age: non-native, introduced to the U.S. from Russia and China; 50-75 years

Habitat: dry soils, sun

Range: throughout, in parks and yards, along roads, old home sites

Stan's Notes: Also called Russian Mulberry, it is so similar to native Red Mulberry (pg. 85) that the only time it is easy to differentiate them is when there is fruit on the trees. Produces abundant berries, which attract birds from miles around. In July and August, when fruit is ripe, the tree is full of activity with birds, squirrels and other animals. Often found growing along fencerows, where perching birds pass seeds through their digestive tracts unharmed. Like the Red Mulberry, leaves exude a milky sap when torn or cut. White Mulberry was introduced in colonial times in an attempt to build a silkworm industry, with large groves planted in the eastern U.S. and southern states.

THORN

BARK

FLOWER

FRUIT

AMERICAN PLUM
Prunus americana

Family:	Rose (Rosaceae)
Height:	10-15' (3-4.5 m)
Tree:	small tree, single trunk, rarely over 6" (15 cm) in diameter, many branches
Leaf:	simple, oblong to oval, 2-5" (5-12.5 cm) in length, alternately attached, pointed tip, double-toothed margin, network of veins, dark green
Bark:	reddish brown or gray to white in color with large light-colored horizontal marks (lenticels), smooth, breaking into large scales or plates, large sharp thorns, 1-3 (2.5-7.5 cm) long
Flower:	showy white flower, 1" (2.5 cm) wide, in clusters, 3-5" (7.5-12.5 cm) wide, very fragrant
Fruit:	large fleshy red plum, edible, 1" (2.5 cm) wide, containing 1 large seed
Fall Color:	golden yellow
Origin/Age:	native; 25-30 years
Habitat:	moist soils, open fields, along edges of woodland, shade intolerant
Range:	southern half and western edge of the state

Stan's Notes: A fast-growing ornamental tree also known as Wild Plum. Shade intolerant, preferring open sunny sites. Flowers are large and attractive. Resulting plums are highly prized by wildlife and people. Plums make good jellies and jams; can be eaten fresh. Very similar to Canada Plum (pg. 91), but differentiated from it by the lack of two small red glands on its leafstalks (petioles). Twigs often smell of bitter almond when crushed. The large sharp thorns (see inset) are actually modified branches. In pioneer times, its thorns were used for mending clothes and other tasks.

THORN

BARK

FLOWER

FRUIT

CANADA PLUM
Prunus nigra

Family: Rose (Rosaceae)

Height: 15-20' (4.5-6 m)

Tree: small tree, short trunk, often crooked and usually divided a few feet up from base, irregular crown

Leaf: simple, oval, 2-5" (5-12.5 cm) length, alternately attached, pointed tip, narrow sharp teeth, dark green, 2 small red swellings (glands) on leafstalk

Bark: dark gray to black when young, becoming brown with age, smooth, breaking into peeling scales, armed with 1-3" (2.5-7.5 cm) long sharp thorns

Flower: 5-petaled white flower, 1" (2.5 cm) wide, growing in clusters, 3-5" (7.5-12.5 cm) wide, fragrant

Fruit: red-to-orange plum, edible, round, 1" (2.5 cm) in diameter, containing 1 large seed

Color: yellow

Origin/Age: native; 25-50 years

Habitat: rich moist soils, river valleys

Range: throughout

Stan's Notes: Entire tree is covered with long sharp thorns (see inset). Very similar to American Plum (pg. 89), but differentiated from it by the red glands on its leafstalks (petioles). Often grows in thickets, sprouting from its roots. Sometimes planted as an ornamental small tree for the wonderful display of white flowers in the spring. Fruit is eaten by wildlife, and ripe plums make great jams or jellies. Occurs in southeastern Canada, hence its common name.

BARK

FLOWER

FRUIT

PIN CHERRY
Prunus pensylvanica

Family: Rose (Rosaceae)

Height: 10-30' (3-9 m)

Tree: single straight or crooked trunk, narrow crown

Leaf: simple, lance-shaped, 2-5" (5-12.5 cm) in length, alternately attached, frequently curved backward, tapering to a point, fine-toothed and often wavy margin, shiny green above and below, 2 small swellings (glands) on the leafstalk near leaf base, leaves often clustered at ends of branches

Bark: gray to nearly black in color, smooth and shiny when young, brown-to-orange marks (lenticels) with age, sometimes peeling into papery strips, pleasant odor when scraped

Flower: 5-petaled white flower, ½" (1 cm) wide, on a long stalk, in clusters, 1-2" (2.5-5 cm) long

Fruit: green cherry, turning bright red at maturity, edible, ¼" (.6 cm) diameter, on a very long red fruit stalk

Fall Color: purplish red

Origin/Age: native; 20-40 years

Habitat: dry soils, open hillsides, fields

Range: throughout

Stan's Notes: Also called Wild Red Cherry, Bird Cherry or Fire Cherry. Common name "Fire" refers to its habit of growing quickly after fires. An important pioneer species, invading openings created by logging, fire or abandoned fields. A great food source for wildlife. The edible cherries are especially good in jellies, and were once used in cough medicines. The long stalks of the flowers and fruit help to distinguish this species from Choke Cherry (pg. 95) and Black Cherry (pg. 97) trees.

BARK

FLOWER

FRUIT

CHOKE CHERRY
Prunus virginiana

Family: Rose (Rosaceae)

Height: 15-35' (4.5-11 m)

Tree: several crooked trunks, irregular crown is usually open with many branches missing

Leaf: simple, oval, 2-5" (5-12.5 cm) length, alternately attached, often is widest above the middle, short sharp tip, fine-toothed margin, shiny green above, lighter below, 2 small swellings (glands) near leaf-stalk (petiole) near leaf base

Bark: dark brown to gray, smooth texture, occasionally with scales, rank odor when scraped or crushed

Flower: 5-petaled white flower, ½" (1 cm) wide, in spike clusters, 2-3" (5-7.5 cm) long, unpleasant odor

Fruit: yellow-to-red cherry, turning nearly black when mature, ¼" (.6 cm) diameter, 6-20 per hanging cluster, ripening in late summer, extremely bitter

Fall Color: yellow, reddish

Origin/Age: native; 25-50 years

Habitat: wide variety of soils, often along fencerows and streams, woodland edges

Range: throughout

Stan's Notes: Appears like a large shrub. Covered with flowers in spring and bitter red-to-black cherries in late summer. Entire plant, except for soft parts of the fruit, contains cyanide, which smells and tastes like bitter almond. Flowers have five petals, like other Rose family members. Birds and other animals eat the fruit. Spread by birds, which void seeds while perching on fences, and by suckers growing from roots, which create large stands. Lacks brown hairs on midrib, as seen on Black Cherry (pg. 97) leaf undersides.

IMMATURE FRUIT

BARK

FRUIT

MIDRIB HAIRS

BLACK CHERRY
Prunus serotina

Family: Rose (Rosaceae)

Height: 50-75' (15-23 m)

Tree: uniformly thick trunk shows little tapering, often tilted or bent, with few lower branches and open round crown

Leaf: simple, lance-shaped, 2-6" (5-15 cm) long, alternately attached, with a unique inward-curved tip resembling a bird's beak, fine-toothed margin, row of fine brown hairs along midrib underneath (see inset), shiny dark green above, paler below

Bark: dark reddish brown to black in color with large, conspicuous curving scales (like potato chips), green inner bark tastes bitter, but smells pleasant

Flower: white flower, ½" (1 cm) wide, 6-12 per elongated cluster, 4-6" (10-15 cm) long

Fruit: green cherry, ¼-½" (.6-1 cm) diameter, turning red to dark blue or black at maturity, edible, in clusters

Fall Color: yellow

Origin/Age: native; 125-150 years

Habitat: wide variety soils, mixed with deciduous species

Range: southern half of state, absent near western border

Stan's Notes: Largest member of the cherry trees. Widely sought for its wonderfully rich brown wood. Several species of *Prunus* in Minnesota, this one producing a tart but edible fruit. An important food crop for birds and wildlife. Bark and roots contain hydrocyanic acid, which has been used in cough medicines and for flavoring. Black knot (a fungus) is the most common disease of Black Cherry, resulting in large black growths along twigs and small branches, leading to die-back of affected branches.

BARK

GINKGO
Ginkgo biloba

Family: Ginkgo (Ginkgoaceae)

Height: 40-60' (12.18 m)

Tree: pyramid shape, single straight trunk and narrow tapering crown

Leaf: simple, fan-shaped, 1-3" (2.5-7.5 cm) wide, alternately attached, 1 or more notches along margin, shallow irregular teeth, no midrib, veins straight and parallel (sometimes forked)

Bark: gray, irregularly rough with many furrows

Fruit: foul-smelling yellow fruit with thick, fleshy outer coat when ripe, 1" (2.5 cm) in diameter, on a long thin fruit stalk

Fall Color: yellow

Origin/Age: non-native, introduced from eastern China; 100-150 years

Habitat: well-drained soils

Range: throughout, in yards and parks, along roads

Stan's Notes: The Ginkgo is the sole surviving species from an ancient family of trees that flourished millions of years ago. Because the surviving trees were cultivated only in ancient temple gardens in China, the species remained unknown to the science community until the late 1700s. Only the male trees are sold and planted since female trees produce butyric acid, which makes the fruit smell foul. Ginkgo fruit has been highly prized by some people for medicinal properties. Its leaves are often in two lobes, hence the species name *biloba*. Also called Maidenhair-tree because the unique fan-shaped leaves resemble the fronds of the Maidenhair Fern plant.

FLOWER

BARK

FRUIT

THORN

RUSSIAN-OLIVE
Elaeagnus angustifolia

Family: Oleaster (Elaeagnaceae)

Height: 10-20' (3-6 m)

Tree: single crooked trunk is often divided low, open irregular crown

Leaf: simple, lance-shaped, 1-4" (2.5-10 cm) in length, alternately attached, blunt tip or sharp tip, margin lacking teeth, gray above and below, leaves and twigs covered with grayish white hairs

Bark: light gray with shallow furrows, thorns on twigs

Flower: 4-petaled yellow flower, ¼-½" (.6-1 cm) wide

Fruit: dry gray-to-yellow olive-like fruit, ¼-½" (.6-1 cm) diameter, containing 1 seed

Fall Color: brown

Origin/Age: non-native, introduced from Europe; 50-75 years

Habitat: wide variety of soils

Range: throughout, formerly planted as an ornamental

Stan's Notes: Was planted in North America for its unusual gray leaves and olive-like fruit, often as a shelterbelt. While it's no longer planted, it has escaped from gardens, yards and parks and now grows in the wild (naturalized). Spread by birds, which pass the seeds through their digestive tracts unharmed. Twigs are often scaly and armed with very long thorns (see inset) that have a salmon-colored pith. The species name *angustifolia* means "narrow leaf." Also called Oleaster or Narrow-leaved Oleaster.

THORN

BARK

FLOWER

FRUIT

HAWTHORN
Crataegus spp.

Family: Rose (Rosaceae)

Height: 15-25' (4.5-7.5 m)

Tree: short round tree, single trunk, flat-topped crown

Leaf: simple, oval to triangular, 2-4" (5-10 cm) length, alternately attached, sometimes 3 lobes, double-toothed margin, thick and shiny, dark green above and below

Bark: gray with red patches, very scaly and covered with peeling bark, sturdy thorns, 1-3" (2.5-7.5 cm) in length, on branches

Flower: 5-petaled white (occasionally pink) flower, 1-2" (2.5-5 cm) diameter, in flat-topped clusters, 3-5" (7.5-12.5 cm) wide, fragrant

Fruit: red (sometimes orange) apple-like fruit, edible, ½-1" (1-2.5 cm) diameter, in clusters

Fall Color: red to orange

Origin/Age: native and non-native; 50-100 years

Habitat: dry soils, open fields, hillsides, sun

Range: throughout

Stan's Notes: One of over 100 species in North America. Because of its affinity to hybridize, there are more than 1,100 different kinds of hawthorn in the U.S. Over a dozen species native to Minnesota with many more introduced, making it difficult to distinguish each. Fruit is edible and eaten by many bird and animal species. Branches and trunk are armed with long sturdy thorns allowing shrikes, also known as Butcher Birds, to impale their prey on the spines. Birds like to construct their nests in this tree, gaining some protection from the large sharp thorns. Also called Thornapple or Haws.

BARK

FLOWER

FRUIT

HACKBERRY
Celtis occidentalis

Family: Elm (Ulmaceae)

Height: 40-60' (12-18 m)

Tree: single trunk, ascending branches with drooping tips, spreading round crown

Leaf: simple, lance-shaped, 2-4" (5-10 cm) long, alternately attached, long tapering tip, asymmetrical leaf base, evenly spaced sharp teeth, hairs on the veins, dark green above, paler below

Bark: unique gray-colored bark is covered with narrow corky ridges, wart-like

Flower: tiny green flower, ⅛" (.3 cm) wide, sprouting from bases of young leaves in early spring

Fruit: green berry-like fruit, turning deep purple when mature, sweet and edible when ripe, ¼" (.6 cm) diameter, containing 1 seed

Fall Color: yellow

Origin/Age: native; 100-150 years

Habitat: wide variety of soils

Range: southern half of the state

Stan's Notes: The very unique corky bark makes this tree easy to identify. In fall, mature trees are laden with dark purple berry-like fruit, which typically doesn't last long because it is a favorite food of many bird species. Fruit can remain on the trees throughout winter if not eaten by birds. Commonly in floodplain forest, but also grows well in dryer areas. Suffers from non-fatal witches'-broom, dense clusters of small short twigs at branch ends caused by the combined efforts of a small insect and a fungus. Often has dimple-like galls on leaves (which do not affect the tree's health) caused by mite insects. Also called Northern Hackberry, Sugarberry or Hack-tree.

BARK

FLOWER

FRUIT

IRONWOOD
Ostrya virginiana

Family: Birch (Betulaceae)

Height: 20-40' (6-12 m)

Tree: single trunk that is often crooked, with spreading branches, open irregular crown

Leaf: simple, oval, 2-4" (5-10 cm) in length, alternately attached, with pointed tip, asymmetrical leaf base, double-toothed margin, fuzzy to touch, yellowish green color

Bark: gray, fibrous with narrow ridges spiraling around the trunk

Flower: catkin, ½-1" (1-2.5 cm) long

Fruit: flattened nutlet, ¼" (.6 cm) wide, within a hanging cluster of inflated sacs that are green when young, turning brown at maturity, 1½-2" (4-5 cm) long, appearing like the fruit of the hop plant

Fall Color: yellow

Origin/Age: native; 75-100 years

Habitat: dry soils, slopes, ridges, shade tolerant

Range: throughout

Stan's Notes: An important understory tree, frequently spending its entire life in the shade of other taller trees. The common name refers to its very strong and heavy wood, which is used to make tool handles and tent stakes. Distinctive thin scaly bark that spirals up the trunk and velvety soft leaves make this tree easy to identify. Also called Hop-hornbeam in direct reference to the fruit sacs, which appear like hops. One of three species of *Ostrya* in North America.

BARK

FLOWER

FRUIT

ALTERNATE-LEAF DOGWOOD
Cornus alternifolia

Family: Dogwood (Cornaceae)

Height: 25-35' (7.5-11 m)

Tree: small understory tree, usually a single trunk with multi-horizontal tiers of branches, resulting in a layered appearance

Leaf: simple, oval, 2-5" (5-12.5 cm) length, alternately attached, pointed tip, margin lacking teeth, deep-curving (arcuate) parallel veins, dark green above, whitish below, leaves are often clustered at ends of the branches

Bark: gray, thin and smooth

Flower: small white-to-cream flower, ¼-½" (.6-1 cm) wide, in round clusters, 3-5" (7.5-12.5 cm) wide

Fruit: green berry-like fruit, turning white to blue to nearly black when mature, round, ¼" (.6 cm) diameter, on a red fruit stalk

Fall Color: red

Origin/Age: native; 40-60 years

Habitat: well-drained open woodland, forest edges, shade

Range: eastern two-thirds of the state

Stan's Notes: A common understory tree that rarely gets taller than 35 feet (11 m), typically cultivated as an ornamental tree for landscaping. Its alternately attached leaves are unique, as other dogwoods have oppositely attached leaves. Branches are distinctly horizontal, growing in tiers, hence another common name, Pagoda Dogwood. "Pagoda" refers to a type of religious building in the Far East which has many stories or levels, just like the many levels of branches on this tree. Look for the clusters of oval leaves near ends of branches.

109

BARK

BLUE BEECH
Carpinus caroliniana

Family: Birch (Betulaceae)

Height: 15-25' (4.5-7.5 m)

Tree: single to multiple crooked trunks, wide and often flat crown

Leaf: simple, oval, 2-5" (5-12.5 cm) length, alternately attached, with pointed tip, asymmetrical leaf base, margin is fine, sharp and double-toothed, color is light green

Bark: light blue-gray to gray, very smooth and unbroken with longitudinal muscle-like ridges

Fruit: many small ribbed nutlets, each ¼" (.6 cm) wide, contained in a leaf-like papery green bract, 2-4" (5-10 cm) long, that hangs in clusters and turns brown when mature

Fall Color: orange to deep red

Origin/Age: native; 50-75 years

Habitat: rich moist soils, moist valleys, along streams and other wet places

Range: southeastern half of the state

Stan's Notes: One of about 25 species of *Carpinus*, Blue Beech is the only native of North America. An easily recognized understory tree, with its smooth unbroken trunk and long, fluted muscle-like ridges. Also known as Musclewood, Water Beech, Ironwood (same common name, but not the Ironwood on pg. 107) or the American Hornbeam. In the latter name, "Horn" means "tough" and "beam" means "tree" in Old English, which describes its tough wood. The wood is used for tool handles.

BARK

FRUIT

SPECKLED ALDER
Alnus rugosa

Family: Birch (Betulaceae)

Height: 15-25' (4.5-7.5 m)

Tree: multiple thin trunks, often crooked, to 6" (15 cm) in diameter, irregular crown

Leaf: simple, oblong, 2-5" (5-12.5 cm) long, alternately attached, double-toothed margin, leathery, veins are sunken, dull green above, pale and often finely hairy below

Bark: dark reddish brown in color, covered with whitish horizontal marks (lenticels), smooth

Flower: catkin, 1-2" (2.5-5 cm) long

Fruit: winged nutlets, each ⅛" (.3 cm) wide, contained in a woody, cone-like seed catkin, ¼-½" (.6-1 cm) in length

Fall Color: dull yellow

Origin/Age: native; 25-50 years

Habitat: wet soils, lake, river and bog edges, shade tolerant

Range: throughout, except for the southwestern quarter

Stan's Notes: A fast-growing, shade-tolerant small tree that usually grows in dense thickets along lakes, streams, ponds and rivers. Well known for its tiny cone-like seed catkins, which are often collected, painted and used as jewelry or in artwork. Its seed catkins are not produced until the tree reaches 8 to 10 years, with abundant crops about every four years after that. The roots have nodules formed by bacteria that converts atmospheric nitrogen into nitrogen in soil, thus improving soil fertility. Young trees sprout from cut stumps. Also called Tag Alder or Gray Alder. Very similar to the Mountain Alder (*A. tenuifolia*) found in the Rocky Mountains.

BARK

FLOWER

FRUIT

EASTERN REDBUD
Cercis canadensis

Family: Caesalpinia (Caesalpiniaceae)

Height: 15-25' (4.5-7.5 m)

Tree: small tree, single or multiple thin trunks with low branching, horizontal branching on umbrella-like spreading crown

Leaf: simple, heart-shaped, 2-6" (5-15 cm) in length, alternately attached, pointed tip, smooth margin, shiny dark green, leafstalk swollen at the top

Bark: gray, smooth with reddish streaks, becoming scaly with age

Flower: pea-like lavender-to-pink flower, ¼" (.6 cm) wide, along the branches

Fruit: reddish brown pod, 2-4" (5-10 cm) long, pointed at both ends, on a short stalk

Fall Color: yellow

Origin/Age: non-native, introduced from eastern and southern North America; 50-75 years

Habitat: moist soils, along streams, forest edges, shade

Range: southern half of the state, in parks and gardens

Stan's Notes: Also known as American Redbud or Judas-tree, the latter name referring to a European legend that this was the species from which Judas hanged himself, and that the once white flowers are now forever red with shame. An understory tree that tolerates shade, it wouldn't be spring in many places without its spectacular display of pink flowers, which appear before the leaves. Only two species in the genus *Cercis* are native to North America, with this one native to southern states.

BARK

FLOWER

FRUIT

AMERICAN BASSWOOD
Tilia americana

Family: Linden (Tiliaceae)

Height: 50-70' (15-21 m)

Tree: tall tree, single or multiple trunks from a common point on the ground, full round crown

Leaf: simple, heart-shaped, 3-7" (7.5-18 cm) in length, alternately attached, with asymmetrical leaf base, sharp-toothed margin, dull green above, lighter green below

Bark: light gray color and smooth when young, darkens with long, narrow flat-topped ridges dividing into a short block with age, inner bark fibrous

Flower: creamy yellow flower, 1-2" (2.5-5 cm) diameter, fragrant odor

Fruit: nut-like green fruit, turning yellow when mature, round, ¼" (.6 cm) diameter, covered with light brown hairs, on a 1-2" (2.5-5 cm) long fruit stalk, hanging in clusters from a leaf-like wing

Fall Color: yellow, orange

Origin/Age: native; 150-200 years

Habitat: moist soils, shade tolerant

Range: throughout

Stan's Notes: A long-lived, fast-growing tree that is well known for growing several trunks from the base of the mother plant. Usually a much shorter life span than 200 years, falling to storm or insect damage. The lightweight soft wood is used for carving due to its smooth grain. From its flowers, bees produce a high quality honey. Fibrous inner bark was once used by American Indians to weave mats, rope and baskets. Also called American Linden or Basswood. Many cultivated varieties exist.

BARK

FRUIT

AMERICAN CHESTNUT
Castanea dentata

Family: Beech (Fagaceae)

Height: 60-90' (18-27.5 m)

Tree: once a tall tree growing to 115' (35 m), but now rarely reaching 30' (9 m) due to chestnut blight, full round crown

Leaf: simple, narrow, 6-12" (15-30 cm) in length, alternately attached, tapering at each end, with unique prominent teeth that extend beyond leaf margin and form a forward curve like the teeth of a saw, straight and parallel veins

Bark: dark brown to red, smooth, separating into wide flat-topped ridges

Flower: catkin with male and female flowers on same tree, male flower in catkin, 1" (2.5 cm) long, solitary female flower, ½" (1 cm) wide, located at base of the catkin

Fruit: bur-like green nut, turning brown at maturity, 2-3" (5-7.5 cm) wide, in clusters, splits into 4 parts

Fall Color: yellow

Origin/Age: non-native; 25-50 years

Habitat: well-drained sandy soils, sun

Range: rarely in the wild, usually seen at dwellings, parks

Stan's Notes: Five native chestnut species in North America, this one producing the proverbial chestnuts roasting over an open fire. Once a large and prominent tree of the eastern U.S., it was nearly wiped out by chestnut blight, a fungus. Grows to half its former size before dying. Hard oak-like wood with a straight grain, relatively decay resistant. Will sprout from stumps of dead or cut trees. The species name *dentata* refers to the obvious large teeth on leaves.

BARK

FLOWER

FRUIT

AMUR MAPLE
Acer ginnala

Family: Maple (Aceraceae)

Height: 15-20' (4.5-6 m)

Tree: small tree to shrub that is often multi-stemmed, with compact lower branches and irregular crown

Leaf: lobed, arrowhead-shaped, 2-4" (5-10 cm) length, oppositely attached, with 3-5 sharp lobes, coarse-toothed, glossy green, leafstalk often bright red

Bark: gray, smooth with many vertical cracks

Flower: small green flower, ½" (1 cm) wide, in drooping clusters, 1-2" (2.5-5 cm) wide

Fruit: pair of red-tinged winged seeds (samara), turning bright red, 1-2" (2.5-5 cm) long

Fall Color: red to orange

Origin/Age: non-native, introduced to the U.S. from eastern Asia; 25-50 years

Habitat: well-drained soils, shade

Range: throughout, planted in parks and yards

Stan's Notes: A remarkably attractive small tree, widely planted as an ornamental shrub for its brilliance in autumn. Very hardy shade-tolerant plant that turns a showy bright red each fall, with winged seeds (samara) also turning bright red. The samaras are often called helicopters due to the way they rotate to the ground. The genus name *Acer* is Latin and means "sharp," referring to its pointed lobes. The common name comes from the Amur River, which forms the boundary between China and Russia, presumably the origin of this species. Also called Siberian Maple.

BARK

FRUIT

MOUNTAIN MAPLE
Acer spicatum

Family: Maple (Aceraceae)

Height: 20-30' (6-9 m)

Tree: small tree with a single crooked trunk and upright branches, irregular crown

Leaf: lobed, 2-4" (5-10 cm) long, oppositely attached, 3 pointed lobes (rarely 5), coarse-toothed margin, light green, leafstalk often red, usually longer than the leaf

Bark: reddish to brown, smooth but grooved with light-colored areas

Flower: many 5-petaled yellowish green flowers, each ½" (1 cm) diameter, growing in spike clusters, 1-3" (2.5-7.5 cm) tall

Fruit: pair of winged seeds (samara), often red, turning yellow, then brown, ¾-1" (2-2.5 cm) long

Fall Color: red or orange

Origin/Age: native; 40-60 years

Habitat: moist soils, along streams and other wet areas, shade tolerant

Range: central and northeastern parts of the state

Stan's Notes: Usually is considered an understory tree because it commonly grows under the canopy of larger, more dominant trees. Doesn't do well in the open. Often grows in rocky outcroppings. Also called Moose Maple since it frequently grows in habitats that are good for moose. The winged seeds are often bright red, later turning yellow, then brown in late summer before falling in early winter. Shallow root system. The wood hasn't been considered for any commercial use.

BARK

FRUIT

RED MAPLE
Acer rubrum

Family: Maple (Aceraceae)

Height: 40-60' (12-18 m)

Tree: single trunk, narrow dense crown

Leaf: lobed, 3-4" (7.5-10 cm) long, oppositely attached, 3-5 lobes (usually 3), shallow notches in between lobes, double-toothed margin, light green color, leafstalk red

Bark: gray, smooth, broken by narrow irregular cracks

Flower: tiny red hanging flower, ¼" (.6 cm) wide, on a 1-2" (2.5-5 cm) long red stalk, growing in clusters, 1-3" (2.5-7.5 cm) wide

Fruit: pair of winged seeds (samara), red in springtime, ½-1" (1-2.5 cm) long

Fall Color: red to orange

Origin/Age: native; 75-100 years

Habitat: wet to moist soils, along swamps or depressions that hold water

Range: northeastern two-thirds of the state

Stan's Notes: One of the most drought-tolerant species of maple in Minnesota. Often planted as an ornamental tree, it can be identified by its characteristic leaves, which have three pointed lobes, and red stalks. The common name comes from the obvious red flowers that bloom early in spring, but the flowers and leafstalks are not the only red colors it has. New leaves, fall color and spring seeds are also red. Produces one of the smallest seeds of any of the maples. Also called Swamp Maple, Water Maple or Soft Maple, the latter common name being the same as the Silver Maple (pg. 131). Even though it is sometimes called Soft Maple, its wood is very hard and brittle.

BARK

FLOWER

FRUIT

SUGAR MAPLE
Acer saccharum

Family: Maple (Aceraceae)

Height: 50-70' (15-21 m)

Tree: single trunk, ascending branches, narrow round to oval crown

Leaf: lobed, 3-5" (7.5-12.5 cm) in length, oppositely attached, 5 lobes (occasionally 3), pointed tips, few irregular teeth, wavy margin, yellowish green above, paler below

Bark: gray in color, narrow furrows and irregular ridges, can be scaly

Flower: greenish yellow flower, ¼" (.6 cm) wide, dangling on a 1-2" (2.5-5 cm) long stalk

Fruit: pair of green winged seeds (samara), turning tan, ¾-1½" (2-4 cm) long

Fall Color: orange to red

Origin/Age: native; 150-200 years

Habitat: rich moist soils

Range: eastern half of state, in yards, parks, along roads

Stan's Notes: A popular and well-known tree, Sugar Maples are the source of maple syrup and maple sugar. It takes approximately 40 gallons (152 L) of sap to make a single gallon of syrup. Any break in a twig, branch or trunk leaks sugary water in spring, attracting birds, bugs and mammals, which lap up the sap. Leaves that have fallen break down quickly, making it one of the best natural and organic fertilizers. Also known as Hard Maple, its extremely hard wood is used in furniture, flooring and cabinets. Often planted in yards, parks and along roads in addition to growing naturally in the eastern half of the state. Closely resembles Black Maple (pg. 129).

BARK

FRUIT

BLACK MAPLE
Acer nigrum

Family: Maple (Aceraceae)

Height: 40-70' (12-21 m)

Tree: medium tree, nearly identical to the Sugar Maple, broad round crown

Leaf: lobed, 3-6" (7.5-15 cm) long, oppositely attached, 3 pointed lobes (rarely 5), with a smooth to wavy margin, dark green above, yellowish below, leaves appear to droop

Bark: light gray, smooth, can get scaly with age

Fruit: pair of green winged seeds (samara), turning tan, 1-2" (2.5-5 cm) long

Fall Color: yellow

Origin/Age: native; 150-175 years

Habitat: moist fertile soils, floodplains, bottomlands, shade

Range: southeastern quarter of the state

Stan's Notes: Nearly identical to the Sugar Maple (pg. 127), with several areas of differentiation. Common name "Black" refers to its bark, which is not black but often is darker than Sugar Maple bark. Leaves occasionally have dense, velvety brownish hairs underneath, sometimes also have a characteristic wilted appearance and turn yellow in fall rather than red, like Sugar Maple leaves. Black Maple trees grow in moister soils and are more drought tolerant and slower growing than Sugar Maples, but they breed easily with each other. Seeds laying in soil remain viable for many years. Because Black and Sugar Maples are so similar, some think they should be considered subspecies, not separate species.

BARK

FLOWER

FRUIT

SILVER MAPLE
Acer saccharinum

Family: Maple (Aceraceae)

Height: 75-100' (23-30.5 m)

Tree: single trunk, ascending branches, open crown

Leaf: lobed, 4-6" (10-15 cm) long, oppositely attached, 5-7 lobes, pointed tips, deep notches and double-toothed margin, dull green above with a silvery white color below

Bark: gray and smooth when young, becomes furrowed, long scaly strips, often peeling and curling at ends

Flower: tiny red dangling flower, ¼" (.6 cm) wide, on a 1-2" (2.5-5 cm) long stalk

Fruit: pair of green winged seeds (samara), turning to brown, 1-2½" (2.5-6 cm) long

Fall Color: yellow to orange

Origin/Age: native; 100-125 years

Habitat: wet to moist soils, often growing in pure stands in floodplains, shade

Range: southern half of the state

Stan's Notes: Usually seen growing in bottomlands or floodplains along rivers where it is often the dominant tree. One of the first trees to bloom (flower) in spring, confusing many to think it is budding early. Bark of older trees is characteristic, with long strips that often peel and curl at ends. Produces heavy seed crops. Also called Silverleaf Maple, its common name coming from the silvery appearance beneath the leaves, and Soft Maple, which is also the same common name of the Red Maple (pg. 125). This name refers to the brittle branches (which often break off in windstorms), rather than to the wood being soft. The wood is actually very hard with a tight grain.

131

FRUIT

BARK

FLOWER

NORWAY MAPLE
Acer platanoides

Family: Maple (Aceraceae)

Height: 40-60' (12-18 m)

Tree: single straight trunk, dense round crown

Leaf: lobed, 5-7" (12.5-18 cm) in length, oppositely attached, 5-7 lobes, shallow notches and a wavy margin, exudes milky sap when cut, shiny dark green above, light green below

Bark: dark gray in color with many narrow furrows and interlacing ridges

Flower: large green flower, ½-¾" (1-2 cm) wide, on a 1-2" (2.5-5 cm) long green stalk

Fruit: pair of widely spread winged seeds (samara), 1-2" (2.5-5 cm) long

Fall Color: yellow, orange

Origin/Age: non-native, introduced to the U.S. from Europe; 100-125 years

Habitat: well-drained rich soils

Range: throughout, planted along streets, in parks

Stan's Notes: This introduced species, most commonly seen along streets and in parks, has spread to wild environments and is doing well. Considered to be one of the most disease- and insect-resistant species of maple and a potential pest species that could outperform the widely prevalent native maples. While leaves are similar to those of Sugar Maple (pg. 127), several Norway Maple varieties have red or purple leaves. Leaves, buds and twigs exude a milky sap when cut. Winged seeds are more widely spread (see inset) than those of Sugar Maple or Silver Maple (pg. 131). Common name implies it was introduced from Norway.

UNDERSIDE

BARK

WHITE POPLAR
Populus alba

Family: Willow (Salicaceae)

Height: 40-60' (12-18 m)

Tree: medium-sized tree with single or multiple trunks, open widely spreading crown

Leaf: lobed, maple-shaped, 2-5" (5-12.5 cm) in length, alternately attached, 3 pointed lobes, few rounded teeth, light green above and chalky white below, covered with white hairs, silky white when young

Bark: dark brown color and deeply furrowed near base, yellowish white color with dark horizontal marks (lenticels) and smooth upper

Flower: catkin, 2-3" (5-7.5 cm) long, composed of many tiny flowers, ¼" (.6 cm) wide

Fruit: catkin-like fruit, 2-3" (5-7.5 cm) long, composed of many capsules that open and release many tiny cottony seeds, which float on the wind

Fall Color: yellow to brown

Origin/Age: non-native, introduced to the U.S. from Europe; 100-125 years

Habitat: wide variety of soils, sun

Range: throughout, in parks and yards, along roads

Stan's Notes: The maple-like lobed leaves of the White Poplar are unusual for a member of the *Populus* genus. Its buds and undersides of its leaves are covered with tiny white hairs, giving newly budded leaves a whitish-colored appearance, and the species its common name. Also known as Silver-leaf Poplar or European White Poplar, it was among the first trees that were introduced to North America from Europe during colonial times. A fast-growing tree with several varieties sold. Its species name *alba* means "white."

BARK

FLOWER

FRUIT

NORTHERN PIN OAK
Quercus ellipsoidalis

Family: Beech (Fagaceae)

Height: 40-60' (12-18 m)

Tree: medium-sized tree with a single trunk, drooping branches and open irregular crown

Leaf: lobed, 4-6" (10-15 cm) long, alternately attached, up to 7 narrow lobes, each ending in a pointed tip (bristle-tipped), deep spaces (sinuses) in between the lobes cutting nearly to midrib, shiny green

Bark: dark brown with shallow furrows and flat ridges

Flower: green-to-red catkin, 1-4" (2.5-10 cm) long, made up of many tiny flowers, ⅛" (.3 cm) wide

Fruit: green acorn, turns brown, edible, ½-1" (1-2.5 cm) long, elongated cap covers upper third of nut

Fall Color: deep red to reddish brown

Origin/Age: native; 100-150 years

Habitat: dry sandy soils, sun

Range: southern half of the state

Stan's Notes: One of over 600 species of oak in the world, with about 60 occurring in the U.S. Also called Hills Oak, it is frequently found growing on dry sandy hillsides. The flowers are pollinated in the first year, but the nuts don't mature until autumn of the second year. Will produce heavy fruit crops every four to six years. Fruit is eaten by wildlife. Acorns contain tannic acid (tannin), which can be toxic in large amounts. Acorns should be processed by boiling in water before eating. Susceptible to oak wilt, a fungus that can kill entire stands of trees. Very similar to the Pin Oak (*Q. palustris*) (not shown), a non-native species of mid-Atlantic states that has deeper, wider sinuses between the leaf lobes.

BARK

FLOWER

FRUIT

SWAMP WHITE OAK
Quercus bicolor

Family: Beech (Fagaceae)

Height: 40-60' (12-18 m)

Tree: single trunk, crooked lower branches and narrow irregular crown

Leaf: lobed, 4-7" (10-18 cm) long, alternately attached, widest above the middle, with shallow lobes that occasionally appear like teeth, dark green above, paler below with white hairs, obvious difference between upper and lower leaf surfaces

Bark: light gray, many vertical furrows, wide flat ridges

Flower: thin catkin, 1-4" (2.5-10 cm) long, composed of hairy green flowers

Fruit: green acorn, turning brown, edible, ¾-1¼" (2-3 cm) long, solitary but can be in pairs, knobby cap covering the upper half of nut

Fall Color: brown

Origin/Age: native; 150-200 years

Habitat: moist soils, along river bottoms, wetland edges

Range: along major riverways in the southeastern quarter

Stan's Notes: A common, fast-growing oak of moist soils. Its acorns, which mature in one season and usually grow in pairs on a long stalk, sprout soon after they fall from the tree in late summer and autumn. Leaf lobes are shallow, unlike the deeply lobed leaves typical of other members of the white oak group such as the White Oak (pg. 141) and Bur Oak (pg. 147). Also called Bicolor Oak (from the species name *bicolor*), which refers to its distinctly different upper and lower leaf surfaces. The crooked lower branches tend to hang down, giving it a messy appearance. Does very well as a landscape plant. Its hard, durable wood has been used in making furniture.

FRUIT

BARK

FLOWER

WHITE OAK
Quercus alba

Family: Beech (Fagaceae)

Height: 50-70' (15-21 m)

Tree: single straight trunk, some gnarled and twisted branches reach toward the ground, broad crown

Leaf: lobed, 4-8" (10-20 cm) long, alternately attached, usually widest above middle, 5-9 rounded lobes, notches deeply cut or shallow and uniform in size and depth, lacks teeth, bright green above, paler below, leaves often clustered at ends of branches

Bark: light gray, broken into reddish scales

Flower: green catkin, 1-3" (2.5-7.5 cm) long, composed of many tiny flowers, ⅛" (.3 cm) wide

Fruit: green acorn, turns brown, edible, ½-1½" (1-4 cm) long, cap covers the upper third of nut

Fall Color: red brown

Origin/Age: native; 150-250 years

Habitat: variety of soils

Range: southern half of the state

Stan's Notes: A very important tree in the lumber industry, with its wood used for furniture, flooring, whiskey barrels, crates and much more. Similar to the Bur Oak (pg. 147), which has a single large terminal lobe unlike White Oak's finger-like lobes. Produces edible acorns each fall, with large crops produced every four to ten years. Like all other acorns, these should be boiled in several changes of water to leech out the bitter and slightly toxic tannins before eating. Acorns are an important food source for turkeys; squirrels, grouse, deer and other wildlife. Susceptible to oak wilt, causing gradual death. Oaks in the white oak group can be treated for oak wilt, while oaks in the red oak group die quickly from the disease.

BARK

FRUIT

BLACK OAK
Quercus velutina

Family: Beech (Fagaceae)

Height: 40-60' (12-18 m)

Tree: medium-sized tree, lower branches are ascending before maturity and horizontal at maturity, upper branches ascending, broad round crown

Leaf: lobed, 4-9" (10-22.5 cm) in length, alternately attached, 5-7 lobes, each ending in a pointed tip (bristle-tipped) and separated by deep U-shaped sinuses, shiny green above and yellowish brown color below

Bark: shiny dark gray and smooth texture when young, becoming nearly black with deep reddish cracks

Flower: light yellow catkin, 1-3" (2.5-7.5 cm) long, made up of many tiny flowers, ⅛" (.3 cm) wide

Fruit: green acorn, turning brown, ¾" (2 cm) long, almost as wide as long with thin black vertical lines on hulls, cap covering the upper half of nut

Fall Color: orange brown

Origin/Age: native; 175-200 years

Habitat: dry sandy soils, steep slopes, sun

Range: southeastern quarter of the state

Stan's Notes: Two oak groups, red and white, with the Black Oak a member of the red oak group. Acorns of the red oak group mature in two seasons, while white oak group acorns mature in one season. Heavy fruit crops only infrequently. Nuts are yellow and very bitter due to tannic acid (tannin). Bark also contains tannin, which was used in tanning animal skins. New leaves unfurling in the spring are crimson before turning silvery, then dark green. Highly susceptible to oak wilt disease.

143

BARK

FLOWER

FRUIT

NORTHERN RED OAK
Quercus rubra

Family: Beech (Fagaceae)

Height: 50-70' (15-21 m)

Tree: single straight trunk, broad round crown

Leaf: lobed, 4-9" (10-22.5 cm) in length, alternately attached, 7-11 lobes, each lobe ending in several pointed tips (bristle-tipped), with sinuses cutting only halfway to midrib, tufts of hair on the veins underneath, dull yellow green

Bark: dark gray color and smooth texture when young, becomes light gray with age, deeply furrowed with flat narrow ridges

Flower: green catkin, 1-4" (2.5-10 cm) long, composed of many tiny flowers, ⅛" (.3 cm) wide

Fruit: green acorn, turning brown, ½-1" (1-2.5 cm) long, on a short stalk, cap covering only the upper quarter of nut

Fall Color: red to brown

Origin/Age: native; 100-150 years

Habitat: moist soils, also does well in dry soils

Range: eastern half of the state

Stan's Notes: A member of the red oak group. Wood is reddish brown, giving the tree the species name *rubra*, meaning "red," as well as the common name, Red Oak. Differentiated from the other red oaks by the leaf sinuses between lobes cutting only halfway to midrib. The pointed leaves and acorns that mature in two seasons distinguish it from the white oak group, which has rounded leaves and acorns that mature in one season. Its bitter-tasting nuts are not popular with wildlife. Succumbs to oak wilt, dying a few weeks after infection. Wood is used in flooring, furniture and many other products.

BARK

FLOWER

FRUIT

BUR OAK
Quercus macrocarpa

Family: Beech (Fagaceae)

Height: 50-80' (15-24.5 m)

Tree: tall straight trunk, distinct nearly to top, branches and twigs thick, nearly horizontal lower branches, upper branches ascending, broad round crown

Leaf: lobed, 5-12" (12.5-30 cm) in length, alternately attached, 7-9 rounded lobes, last (terminal) lobe often the largest, margin lacking teeth, shiny dark green, leaves clustered near ends of twigs

Bark: dark gray, deeply furrowed, many ridges, scales

Flower: green catkin, 1-3" (2.5-7.5 cm) long, composed of many tiny flowers, ⅛" (.3 cm) wide

Fruit: green acorn, turning brown, sweet and edible, 1-2" (2.5-5 cm) long, cap with hairy edge covering more than upper half of nut

Fall Color: yellow or brown

Origin/Age: native; 150-250 years

Habitat: deep rich soils, drought and shade tolerant

Range: throughout

Stan's Notes: The largest eastern oak, found between prairie and woodland. Thick corky bark allows it to withstand fires. Member of the white oak group (leaves have rounded lobes; acorns mature in one season). Leaves highly variable but lobes are always rounded, with the terminal lobe the largest. Species name is Latin, with *macro* for "large" and *carpa* for "finger," referring to the large terminal leaf lobe. Heavy fruit crops every three to five years, depending on weather. Sweet, edible acorns frequently contain Nut Weevil larvae. Often has oak gall, a fleshy, swollen, round deformity caused by a kind of wasp larvae. Also called Blue Oak or Mossycup Oak.

FRUIT

BARK

WHITE ASH
Fraxinus americana

Family: Olive (Oleaceae)

Height: 40-60' (12-18 m)

Tree: medium-sized tree with single straight trunk and narrow, open round crown

Leaf: compound, 8-12" (20-30 cm) length, oppositely attached, composed of 7 (occasionally 5-9) oval leaflets, each leaflet 3-5" (7.5-12.5 cm) long, with few teeth or toothless, dark green above, distinctly whiter in color below, on a leaflet stalk (petiolule), ¼-½" (.6-1 cm) long

Bark: greenish gray with many furrows and interlacing diamond-shaped ridges

Fruit: green winged seed (samara), turning brown when mature, 1-2" (2.5-5 cm) long, notched or rounded wing tip, remaining on tree into winter

Fall Color: bronze purple

Origin/Age: native; 150-200 years

Habitat: well-drained upland soils, sun

Range: southeastern quarter of the state

Stan's Notes: Very similar to the Green Ash (pg. 151), but tends to grow in sunny, dry, well-drained upland sites. It is by far the most abundant of all 16 ash tree species in the U.S. The largest of the six ash tree species in eastern states, it is also fast growing, able to reach a height of up to 10 feet (3 m) in just under five years. Produces seeds every year and unusually large masses of seeds every two to five years. Young sprouts emerge from stumps or after fire damage. Common name "White" refers to the pale undersides of the leaves. The straight narrow-grained wood is used to make tennis racquets, baseball bats, snowshoes and hockey sticks.

BARK

FRUIT

GREEN ASH
Fraxinus pennsylvanica

Family: Olive (Oleaceae)

Height: 50-60' (15-18 m)

Tree: single straight trunk with ascending branches and irregular crown

Leaf: compound, 9-16" (22.5-40 cm) long, oppositely attached, made of 5-9 stalked leaflets, each leaflet 1-2" (2.5-5 cm) long, lacking teeth or with a very fine-toothed margin, on a very short leaflet stalk (petiolule), $\frac{1}{8}$" (.3 cm) long

Bark: brown with deep furrows and narrow interlacing ridges, often appearing diamond-shaped

Fruit: green winged seed (samara), turning brown when mature, 1-2" (2.5-5 cm) in length, mostly round-ended, sometimes notched, in clusters, frequently remaining on tree into winter

Fall Color: yellow

Origin/Age: native; 75-100 years

Habitat: wet soils, along streams, lowland forest, shade

Range: throughout

Stan's Notes: By far the most widespread of all of our Minnesota ash trees, found throughout the state. Also called Red Ash because it was once thought that the green and red were separate species. Now considered one species. Not as water tolerant as the Black Ash (pg. 153), but able to survive with its roots under water for several weeks early in spring. Often has a large unattractive growth (insect gall) at ends of small branches that persists on the tree throughout the year. The strong white-colored wood is used to make baseball bats, tennis racquets, skis and snowshoes.

BARK

FLOWER

FRUIT

BLACK ASH
Fraxinus nigra

Family: Olive (Oleaceae)

Height: 40-50' (12-15 m)

Tree: tall slender tree, slender trunk is often leaning or bent, upright branches, open narrow crown

Leaf: compound, 9-17" (22.5-40 cm) long, oppositely attached, made of 7-13 narrow tapered leaflets, each leaflet 3-5" (7.5-12.5 cm) long, with pointed tip, fine-toothed margin, yellowish green, lacking a leaflet stalk (sessile)

Bark: light gray, becoming corky with ridges coming off like scales, soft enough to indent with a fingernail, flaking off when rubbed

Flower: green flower, ⅛" (.3 cm) wide, in loose clusters

Fruit: green winged seed (samara), turning brown when mature, 1-2" (2.5-5 cm) long, in clusters, often remaining on tree well into winter

Fall Color: yellow and brown

Origin/Age: native; 100-125 years

Habitat: wet soils, floodplains, can tolerate standing water for several weeks, shade intolerant

Range: throughout, except for the western edge

Stan's Notes: Produces a good seed crop every five to seven years, with seeds usually germinating two years after falling from the tree. Sixteen species of ash in North America, six found east of the Rocky Mountains. Black Ash leaflets are not stalked, as are the leaflets of other ash species. Also called Swamp Ash because it often grows at water's edge. Known as Basket Ash or Hoop Ash because the fresh green wood cut into strips was used to weave baskets, and make snowshoe frames and canoe ribs.

FRUIT

BARK

FLOWER

BOXELDER
Acer negundo

Family: Maple (Aceraceae)

Height: 30-50' (9-15 m)

Tree: medium-sized tree, frequently with a divided and crooked trunk, broad irregular crown

Leaf: compound, 4-9" (10-22.5 cm) length, oppositely attached, made of 3-5 leaflets, each leaflet 2-4" (5-10 cm) in length, often 3-lobed, irregular-toothed margin, pale green

Bark: light gray to tan, becoming deeply furrowed with wavy ridges

Flower: tiny reddish flower, ¼" (.6 cm) wide, growing on a 1-3" (2.5-7.5 cm) long stalk

Fruit: pair of green winged seeds (samara), turning to brown, 1-2" (2.5-5 cm) long

Fall Color: yellow

Origin/Age: native; 50-60 years

Habitat: wet, along streams, lakes and flooded areas, sun

Range: throughout

Stan's Notes: One of the most common trees in the state. Unique among native maple trees because its leaves are compound. A member of the Maple family with all the virtues, but none of the respect. Often thought of as a trash tree, but produces large amounts of seeds which remain on the tree throughout the winter, making a valuable food source for wildlife. If the tree is tapped in spring, it will yield a sap that can be boiled into maple syrup. Since its sugar content is lower than that of other maples, it takes more sap to make a comparable syrup. Trees are often covered with Boxelder Bugs, harmless beetles whose larvae eat the leaves but cause little damage. Also called Manitoba Maple or Ash-leaved Maple.

FRUIT

BARK

AMUR CORK-TREE
Phellodendron amurense

Family: Rue (Rutaceae)

Height: 30-50' (9-15 m)

Tree: medium-sized tree that has a single straight trunk, many low spreading branches and round crown

Leaf: compound, 6-12" (15-30 cm) length, oppositely attached, composed of 5-13 lance-shaped leaflets, each leaflet 2-4" (5-10 cm) long, with pointed tip, wavy margin that lacks teeth, shiny dark green, leaflet stalk (petiolule) yellow, central stalk (rachis) dark brown

Bark: light gray, many coarse, irregular-shaped fissures revealing a reddish inner cork bark

Fruit: green berry-like fruit, turning dark blue in color and aromatic when mature, ½" (1 cm) diameter, containing 5 seeds

Fall Color: yellow

Origin/Age: non-native, introduced from eastern Asia (China) in the mid-1800s; 100-125 years

Habitat: well-drained moist soils, sun

Range: throughout, planted in parks and around homes, along boulevards

Stan's Notes: Attractive, medium-sized cultivated tree, moderately shade intolerant. Its genus name comes from the Greek *phellos*, meaning "cork," and *dendron*, meaning "tree," and refers to its bark. The species name *amurense* refers to its place of origin, the Amur Valley in Manchuria. Considered a pest tree in some areas of North America. Male and female flowers grow on separate trees; only the female trees bear fruit. Berry-like fruit remains on tree into winter and is eaten by wildlife. Central stalks have large yellowish spots (lenticels), which allow air to enter the interior of the plant.

BARK

FLOWER

FRUIT

EUROPEAN MOUNTAIN-ASH
Sorbus aucuparia

Family: Rose (Rosaceae)

Height: 15-25' (4.5-7.5 m)

Tree: single trunk, ascending branches, round crown

Leaf: compound, 4-8" (10-20 cm) in length, alternately attached, made of 9-17 oval leaflets, each leaflet 1-2" (2.5-5 cm) long, with fine-toothed margin, dull green above, whitish below, central stalk (rachis) often yellowish

Bark: shiny gray in color, smooth with many horizontal lines (lenticels)

Flower: greenish flower, ¼" (.6 cm) wide, in flat clusters, 3-5" (7.5-12.5 cm) wide

Fruit: orange or red berry-like fruit, ¼" (.6 cm) diameter, in hanging clusters, 3-5" (7.5-12.5 cm) long, 1-2 shiny black seeds per fruit

Fall Color: yellow

Origin/Age: non-native, introduced from Europe; 25-50 years

Habitat: dry soils, sun

Range: throughout, in yards and parks, along roads

Stan's Notes: A member of the Rose family and not a type of ash tree, it is by far the most commonly planted type of mountain-ash tree. Nearly identical to American Mountain-ash (pg. 161), except for yellowish central stalk. Often a favorite tree of Yellow-bellied Sapsuckers. Spread by birds passing seeds through their digestive tracts unharmed. Latin species name *aucuparia* comes from *avis* and *capere*, meaning "to catch birds," suggesting the fruit was used to bait bird traps. The berry-like fruit provides a good source of food for birds and other wildlife. Containing high amounts of vitamin C, it was once used to cure scurvy. Also called Rowan-tree.

BARK

FLOWER

FRUIT

AMERICAN MOUNTAIN-ASH
Sorbus americana

Family: Rose (Rosaceae)

Height: 15-30' (4.5-9 m)

Tree: small tree, often shrub-like with multiple trunks, open round crown

Leaf: compound, 6-9" (15-22.5 cm) length, alternately attached, made up of 11-17 lance-shaped leaflets, each leaflet 2-4" (5-10 cm) long, fine sharp teeth, pale green, central stalk (rachis) often reddish

Bark: light gray color, many elongated horizontal lines (lenticels), smooth, becoming very scaly with age

Flower: white-to-cream flower, ¼" (.6 cm) wide, in flat clusters, 3-5" (7.5-12.5 cm) wide

Fruit: bright orange or red berry-like fruit, ¼" (.6 cm) diameter, in clusters, 3-5" (7.5-12.5 cm) wide

Fall Color: yellow

Origin/Age: native; 25-50 years

Habitat: cool moist sites, wetland and forest edges, rocky hillsides, shade

Range: northeastern part of the state, Arrowhead region

Stan's Notes: An understory tree of northern forests that doesn't grow well in southern Minnesota. Sun intolerant, this slow-growing ornamental tree is susceptible to fire blight disease and sunscald. Widely planted in landscapes because of its showy flowers and the resulting brightly colored fruit. A favorite forage of moose and deer. Often a favorite tree of Yellow-bellied Sapsuckers, which drill rows of horizontal holes and lap up the resulting sap. Birds, especially Cedar Waxwings and Ruffed Grouse, consume the berry-like fruit. Cultivated varieties are often planted to attract birds. Worldwide there are about 75 species of mountain-ash.

FLOWER

BARK

FRUIT

POISON-SUMAC
Toxicodendron vernix

Family: Cashew (Anacardiaceae)

Height: 5-20' (1.5-6 m)

Tree: small tree, single trunk, few horizontal branches, open irregular crown

Leaf: compound, 6-12" (15-30 cm) length, alternately attached, composed of 7-13 lance-shaped leaflets, each leaflet 1½-3" (4-7.5 cm) long, lacking teeth, smooth to touch, dark green above, pale white in color below, leaflet stalk (petiolule) and central stalk (rachis) often reddish

Bark: light gray, smooth

Flower: green flower, ¼" (.6 cm) wide, in clusters, 2-4" (5-10 cm) wide, on open branches

Fruit: green-to-glossy-white berry-like fruit, ¼" (.6 cm) diameter, remaining on tree into winter

Fall Color: yellow to red

Origin/Age: native; 50-75 years

Habitat: wet soils, bogs, sun

Range: scattered through central and southeastern parts of the state

Stan's Notes: The only sumac of the three species growing in the state that is poisonous. A rare tree found only in open swamps and bogs. Few, if any, encounter this tree due to its remote wet habitat and rarity of species. The oils of Poison-Sumac are toxic, causing severe skin rash. If burned, the smoke can cause severe breathing difficulties, irritated eyes and skin. Closely related to our other sumacs (pp. 165 and 167) and to Poison-ivy. No Poison-oak occurs in Minnesota.

FLOWER

BARK

FRUIT

SMOOTH SUMAC
Rhus glabra

Family: Cashew (Anacardiaceae)

Height: 10-20' (3-6 m)

Tree: multiple trunks, closed flat-topped crown

Leaf: compound, 12-24" (30-60 cm) length, alternately attached, composed of 11-31 leaflets, each leaflet 2-4" (5-10 cm) long, toothed margin, dark green above, some red hairs below, lacking a leaflet stalk (sessile), attaching directly to central stalk (rachis)

Bark: brown, smooth, rarely any furrows or scales

Flower: green flower, ¼" (.6 cm) diameter, in open wide upright clusters, 4-8" (10-20 cm) tall

Fruit: red berry-like fruit, ⅛" (.3 cm) diameter, in cone-shaped clusters, 4-8" (10-20 cm) long

Fall Color: red

Origin/Age: native; 25-50 years

Habitat: dry or poor soils, forest edges, sun

Range: throughout

Stan's Notes: One of the first trees to turn colors in fall. Over 100 species of sumac, most occurring in southern Africa. Three species in Minnesota include Poison-Sumac (pg. 163) and Staghorn Sumac (pg. 167). Closely related to the Staghorn Sumac, which has hairy central stalks and leaves. While Smooth Sumac is not as common as Staghorn, they hybridize where occurring together. Fast growing, reproducing by underground roots that send up new trunks. Often forms a dense stand. Once established, it is often hard to eradicate. Has been planted to stabilize slopes from erosion. Separate male and female plants, so not all sumacs produce the attractive clusters of red fruit. Animals and birds eat the berry-like fruit. Historically, a tea was made by soaking clusters of ripe fruit.

FLOWER

BARK

FRUIT

STAGHORN SUMAC
Rhus typhina

Family: Cashew (Anacardiaceae)

Height: 10-20' (3-6 m)

Tree: multiple trunks, closed flat-topped crown

Leaf: compound, 12-24" (30-60 cm) length, alternately attached, composed of 11-31 leaflets, each leaflet 2-4" (5-10 cm) long, with toothed margin, dark green above, red hairs below, lacking a leaflet stalk (sessile), attaching directly to the central stalk (rachis), which is often hairy and reddish

Bark: brown, smooth, rarely any furrows or scales

Flower: green flower, ¼" (.6 cm) diameter, in tight cone-shaped clusters, 4-8" (10-20 cm) long

Fruit: fuzzy red berry-like fruit, ⅛" (.3 cm) diameter, in thin cone-shaped clusters, 4-8" (10-20 cm) long

Fall Color: red to maroon

Origin/Age: native; 25-50 years

Habitat: dry or poor soils, forest edges, sun

Range: throughout, along highways, in parks and yards

Stan's Notes: One of the first trees to turn colors each autumn. Its fuzzy central stalks resemble the velvety antlers of a deer, and give it the common name. Closely related to Smooth Sumac (pg. 165), which lacks hairy leaves and central stalks. While Staghorn Sumac is by far more common than the Smooth, they will hybridize where they occur together. Reproduces by underground roots that send up new trunks. Fast growing, often forming a dense stand extending up to several hundred feet in each direction. Frequently is planted along highways due to its rapid growth, thus stabilizing soil quickly. Animals and birds eat the red berry-like fruit. Seeds soaked in water produce a sour lemonade drink.

THORN

BARK

FRUIT

COMMON PRICKLY-ASH
Zanthoxylum americanum

Family: Rue (Rutaceae)

Height: 5-15' (1.5-4.5 m)

Tree: small tree, single trunk, round crown

Leaf: compound, 5-10" (12.5-25 cm) long, alternately attached, made of 5-11 oval leaflets, each leaflet 1-2" (2.5-5 cm) in length, lacking teeth, citrus odor when crushed, dull green

Bark: gray, smooth with dark gray marks (lenticels) and white blotches, stout sharp thorns on branches

Fruit: green berry-like fruit, turning to bright red when mature, ¼" (.6 cm) diameter, in clusters, splitting open in autumn and releasing the seed, strong orange or lemon-like citrus odor when crushed

Fall Color: yellow

Origin/Age: native; 25-30 years

Habitat: wide variety of soils, along forest edges

Range: throughout

Stan's Notes: One of two members of the Rue (sometimes referred to as Citrus) family in Minnesota. This is a small tree with stout sharp thorns covering its branches. The leaves and especially the berry-like fruit contain zanthoxylin, a citrus-smelling oil. Fruit and inner bark cause numbness in the mouth and have been used for treatment of toothaches, hence its other common name, Toothache Tree. The Greek genus name *Zanthoxylum* means "yellow wood," and describes the wood of this tree. Reproduces from underground roots and forms thick stands along forest edges. Fruit is highly fragrant, smelling like oranges, lemons and limes combined, when crushed.

BARK

FRUIT

BITTERNUT HICKORY
Carya cordiformis

Family: Walnut (Juglandaceae)

Height: 50-100' (15-30.5 m)

Tree: large tree, sturdy straight trunk, slender upright branches, open round crown

Leaf: compound, 6-10" (15-25 cm) length, alternately attached, composed of 7-11 narrow leaflets, each leaflet 3-6" (7.5-15 cm) long, with pointed tip and fine-toothed margin, shiny green above, paler in color below, lacks a leaflet stalk (sessile), attaching directly to the central stalk (rachis)

Bark: gray in color with irregular vertical cracks, scaly in appearance but never loose scales

Fruit: nut, too bitter to be edible, round, ¾-1½" (2-4 cm) diameter, with pointed end, 4 ridges extending to point, yellowish hairs covering outer husk

Fall Color: golden yellow

Origin/Age: native; 100-150 years

Habitat: moist lowlands, shade intolerant

Range: southeastern quarter of the state

Stan's Notes: The most extensive and northerly of hickories, it is slow growing and shade intolerant. Its large, distinctive yellow buds are diagnostic before the leaves emerge. The wood is used to smoke meat and produces the best flavor of all hickories. Meat of the nuts is very bitter and unpalatable to humans and much wildlife, hence the common name. Oil extracted from the nuts was used for lamp fuel. Sometimes called Bitter Pecan because it is closely related to the true pecan. Also called Swamp Hickory due to its preference for wet or loamy soils. Hickories are found naturally in eastern North America and Asia. About 12 species are native to North America.

BARK

FRUIT

TWIG

SHAGBARK HICKORY
Carya ovata

Family: Walnut (Juglandaceae)

Height: 40-60' (12-18 m)

Tree: medium-sized tree with single straight trunk and tall, narrow irregular crown

Leaf: compound, 8-14" (20-36 cm) length, alternately attached, made up of 5 (rarely 7) pointed leaflets, each leaflet 3-4" (7.5-10 cm) long, widest at the middle, upper 3 leaflets larger than lower 2, fine-toothed margin, yellowish green, lacks leaflet stalk (sessile), attaching directly to central stalk (rachis)

Bark: gray in color, long smooth vertical strips curling at each end, giving it a shaggy appearance

Fruit: green nut, turning brown at maturity, inner kernel sweet, edible, round to oval, 1-1½" (2.5-4 cm) in diameter, single or in pairs, thick 4-ribbed husk

Fall Color: yellow

Origin/Age: native; 150-200 years

Habitat: rich moist soils, sun

Range: southeastern quarter of the state

Stan's Notes: Also called Upland Hickory. Often found on hillsides that have rich moist soils, growing branch-free for three-quarters of its height. Its common name comes from the large scaly or "shaggy" bark. Also known as Shell-bark or Seal-bark Hickory. Hickories are divided into two groups: true hickories, which include Shagbark, and pecan hickories, which include Bitternut Hickory (pg. 171) and Pecan Hickory. Shagbark nuts are eaten by wildlife and people. Its extremely hard wood is used for tool handles, skis and wagon wheels. Unlike walnuts, which have a light brown pith, the twigs of this tree have a white pith (see inset).

THORN

BARK

FLOWER

FRUIT

BLACK LOCUST
Robinia pseudoacacia

Family: Pea or Bean (Fabaceae)

Height: 30-50' (9-15 m)

Tree: medium-sized tree, often crooked trunk, upright spreading branches, open irregular crown

Leaf: compound, 7-14" (18-36 cm) length, alternately attached, composed of 7-19 oval to round leaflets, each leaflet 1-2" (2.5-5 cm) in length, lacks teeth, yellowish green

Bark: dark brown color and smooth texture, becoming furrowed and scaly with age, opposite pairs of stout thorns (see inset), especially on young trees

Flower: pea-like white flower with yellow center, ½-1" (1-2.5 cm) wide, in hanging clusters, 2-4" (5-10 cm) long, appearing soon after leaves develop, fragrant

Fruit: green pod, turning brown when mature, flat, 2-4" (5-10 cm) long, containing 4-8 seeds

Fall Color: yellow

Origin/Age: non-native, was introduced to the state from the Appalachian Mountains; 75-100 years

Habitat: moist woods, adapts to almost any type of soil, shade intolerant

Range: throughout, along roads, in parks, around homes

Stan's Notes: Fifteen species of locust trees and shrubs, all native to North America. Wood is so strong that in the 1800s the British credited success of the U.S. naval fleet in the War of 1812 to Black Locust lumber, used to build ships. Roots combine with bacteria, fixing atmospheric nitrogen into the soil. Spreads rapidly by root suckering. Branches and twigs have stout thorns in pairs at bases of leafstalks. Susceptible to Locust Borer beetles, which bore into trunks.

TWIG

BARK

FLOWER

FRUIT

BLACK WALNUT
Juglans nigra

Family: Walnut (Juglandaceae)

Height: 50-75' (15-23 m)

Tree: straight trunk, open round crown

Leaf: compound, 12-24" (30-60 cm) length, alternately attached, composed of 15-23 stalkless leaflets (sessile), each leaflet 3-4" (7.5-10 cm) long, with pointed tip, last (terminal) leaflet often smaller or absent, middle leaflets larger than on either end, fine-toothed margin, yellowish green and smooth above, slightly lighter and hairy below

Bark: brown to black, becoming darker with age, deep pits and flat scaly ridges

Flower: catkin, 2-4" (5-10 cm) long, composed of many tiny green flowers, ¼" (.6 cm) wide

Fruit: fleshy green fruit, round, 1-2" (2.5-5 cm) wide, in clusters, aromatic green husk surrounding a hard dark nut that matures in autumn, nutmeat sweet and edible

Fall Color: yellowish green

Origin/Age: native; 150-175 years

Habitat: well-drained rich soils, shade intolerant

Range: south central and southeastern parts of the state

Stan's Notes: One of six species of walnut native to North America. Valued for its wood, which doesn't shrink or warp and is used to build furniture and cabinets. An important food source for wildlife. Fruit husks contain a substance that stains skin and were used by pioneers to dye clothing light brown. Twigs have a light brown chambered pith (see inset), unlike dark brown pith of Butternut (pg. 179). Fallen leaves and roots produce juglone, a natural herbicide.

IMMATURE
FRUIT

BARK

FRUIT

TWIG

BUTTERNUT
Juglans cinerea

Family: Walnut (Juglandaceae)

Height: 40-60' (12-18 m)

Tree: medium-sized tree, usually a divided trunk, open broad and often flat crown

Leaf: compound, 15-25" (37.5-63 cm) long, alternately attached, made of 11-17 stalkless leaflets (sessile), each leaflet 2-4" (5-10 cm) in length, fine-toothed margin, last (terminal) leaflet usually present and same size as the lateral leaflets, and progressing smaller toward the leaf base, stout hairs covering each leaflet and the central stalk (rachis)

Bark: light gray with broad flat ridges

Flower: catkin, 1-2" (2.5-5 cm) long, composed of many tiny green flowers, ¼" (.6 cm) wide

Fruit: nut, edible, egg-shaped or oval, 2-3" (5-7.5 cm) in length, in clusters, sticky green husk, turns brown

Fall Color: yellow

Origin/Age: native; 80-100 years

Habitat: wide variety of soils, often on slopes having well-drained rich soils, sun

Range: southeastern quarter of the state

Stan's Notes: A short-lived tree, also called White Walnut. Its very hard, strong wood is much sought by woodcarvers. Twigs are stout with a dark brown chambered pith (see inset). The sap can be boiled to make syrup. Yellow dye can be extracted from the husks and used to color fabrics. Common name comes from its butter-like oil, which American Indians once extracted from the nuts. Latin species name *cinerea* means "ash" and describes the color of the bark. Butternut canker, caused by a fungus, has killed many of these trees.

BARK

FLOWER

FRUIT

HONEY-LOCUST
Gleditsia triacanthos

Family: Caesalpinia (Caesalpiniaceae)

Height: 40-60' (12-18 m)

Tree: single trunk is often divided low, open broad and sometimes flat-topped crown

Leaf: twice compound, 12-24" (30-60 cm) long, alternately attached, composed of 14-30 egg-shaped, feathery leaflets, each leaflet 1" (2.5 cm) in length, fine-toothed margin, dark green above and yellow green below

Bark: reddish brown covered with gray horizontal lines (lenticels), often cracking and peeling, frequently thorny on trunk and branches

Flower: small green catkin, 1-2" (2.5-5 cm) long

Fruit: large pea-like pod, purple brown, flat, twisted, 6-16" (15-40 cm) long, 12-14 oval seeds per pod

Fall Color: yellow

Origin/Age: native; 100-125 years

Habitat: moist or rich soils, sun

Range: southeastern Minnesota, at parks, yards and roads

Stan's Notes: Also called Thorny-locust because it has large thorns on the trunk and branches, and twigs are zigzagged with thorns at the joints. Between the seeds in the seedpods is a sweet yellowish substance, hence "Honey" in the common name. Large and obvious seedpods are eaten by wildlife. Shouldn't be pruned in wet weather as it opens the tree to infection by nectria canker. Thornless and seedless varieties are widely planted in parks and yards, and along roads. Most varieties planted in landscaping lack thorns and fruit. Largest of the two species of *Gleditsia* native to North America.

BARK

FRUIT

KENTUCKY COFFEETREE
Gymnocladus dioicus

Family: Caesalpinia (Caesalpiniaceae)

Height: 40-60' (12-18 m)

Tree: single trunk, can be divided low, many crooked branches, open round crown

Leaf: twice compound, 12-36" (30-90 cm) long, alternately attached, made of many (up to 70) leaflets, each leaflet 2" (5 cm) long, lacks teeth, blue green

Bark: brown and smooth when young, thin scales with edges curling out, breaking with age into plates

Flower: 5-petaled white flower, ¼-½" (.6-1 cm) diameter, on a single long stalk, in open clusters, 1-3" (2.5-7.5 cm) wide

Fruit: leathery green pod, turning reddish brown when mature, 4-10" (10-25 cm) in length, often covered with a whitish powder, containing 6-9 large seeds

Fall Color: yellow

Origin/Age: native; 50-75 years

Habitat: deep rich soils, sun

Range: river valleys in southeastern quarter and scattered throughout, urban sites, farms, parks, along roads

Stan's Notes: Rare native tree that doesn't grow to its full capacity in Minnesota due to weather. Leaves are among the last to appear in spring, first to turn in fall. Common name comes from its coffee-like bean in seedpods. Seedpods contain dark seeds surrounded by a yellowish pulp that becomes soapy when wet. The bitter seeds are seldom eaten by wildlife and remain viable for several years. New trees sprout from roots of parent trees, often forming small colonies. The genus name *Gymnocladus* comes from the Greek for "naked branch," which is how the branches appear.

BARK

FLOWER

FRUIT

HORSE-CHESTNUT
Aesculus hippocastanum

Family: Horse-chestnut (Hippocastanaceae)

Height: 40-60' (12-18 m)

Tree: medium-sized tree with single trunk that is often divided low, spreading round crown

Leaf: palmate compound, 5-10" (12.5-25 cm) length, oppositely attached, composed of 5-9 (usually 7) leaflets, each leaflet 4-10" (10-25 cm) long, widest above the middle, radiating from a central point, with a sharp-toothed margin, hairy below when young, lacking hairs when mature

Bark: dark brown, many furrows and scales, inner bark orange brown

Flower: white flower with yellow or orange center, ½-1" (1-2.5 cm) wide, upright in spike clusters, 8-12" (20-30 cm) long

Fruit: thick-walled leathery green capsule, rounded, 2" (5 cm) diameter, covered with pointed spines, in hanging clusters, splits in 3 sections, contains 1-3 smooth, non-edible, shiny chestnut-brown seeds

Fall Color: yellow

Origin/Age: non-native, introduced to the U.S. from Europe; 75-100 years

Habitat: wide variety of soils

Range: throughout, planted in parks and yards

Stan's Notes: Closely related to Ohio Buckeye (pg. 187). A remedy made from the seeds was used to treat cough in horses, hence its species and common names, *Hippo* ("Horse") and *Kastanon* ("chestnut"). The chemical esculin has been extracted from its leaves and bark for use in skin protectants. Also called Chestnut.

FRUIT

BARK

FLOWER

OHIO BUCKEYE
Aesculus glabra

Family: Horse-chestnut (Hippocastanaceae)

Height: 20-40' (6-12 m)

Tree: single trunk, broad round crown with flat top

Leaf: palmate compound, 5-15" (12.5-37.5 cm) long, oppositely attached, composed of 5 leaflets, each leaflet 3-5" (7.5-12.5 cm) long, radiating from a central point, with fine irregular teeth, yellowish green above, pale color and hairy below, lacking a leaflet stalk (sessile)

Bark: brown with scaly patches, rough shallow furrows

Flower: green flower, ½" (1 cm) wide, growing upright in triangular clusters, 5-7" (12.5-18 cm) long, foul smelling when crushed

Fruit: light brown spiny capsule, round, 1-2" (2.5-5 cm) wide, contains 1-2 shiny brown poisonous seeds

Fall Color: yellow to orange

Origin/Age: non-native, introduced to Minnesota from eastern states; 100-125 years

Habitat: moist soils, river bottoms

Range: throughout, in parks and yards, along streets

Stan's Notes: Also known as Fetid Buckeye or Stinking Buckeye, referring to the foul smell of the flowers and most other parts of the tree when crushed. Grows naturally in moist areas. Planted as a landscape tree in dry upland areas for its attractive autumn foliage. Its large poisonous seeds are avoided by wildlife. A unique palmate leaf, the leaflets lacks their own leafstalks, all rising instead from a central stalk. An extract from the bark was once used as a stimulant for the cerebrospinal system. Once thought a buckeye seed carried in the pocket would ward off rheumatism.

CHECK LIST/INDEX

Use the boxes to check trees you've seen.

GLOSSARY

Acorn: A nut, typically of oak trees, as in the White Oak. See *nut* and *fruit*.

Aggregate fruit: A fruit composed of multiple tiny berries, such as a mulberry, raspberry or blackberry. See *fruit*.

Alternate: A type of leaf attachment in which the leaves are singly and alternately attached along a stalk, as in Balsam Poplar.

Arcuate: Curved in form, like a bow, as in veins of Alternate-leaf Dogwood leaves.

Asymmetrical leaf base: A base of a leaf with lobes unequal in size or shape, as in elms. See *leaf base*.

Berry: A fleshy fruit with several seeds within, such as European Buckthorn. See *fruit*.

Bract: A petal-like structure on a flower, as in Blue Beech.

Branch: The smaller, thinner, woody parts of a tree, usually bearing the leaves and flowers.

Bristle-tipped: A type of leaf lobe ending in a projection, usually a sharply pointed tip, as in Northern Red Oak.

Capsule: A dry fruit that opens along several seams to release the seeds within, as in Ohio Buckeye. See *pod*.

Catkin: A scaly cluster of usually same sex flowers, as in Bigtooth Aspen or any willow.

Chambered pith: The central soft part of a twig that is broken into spaced sections. See *pith*.

Clasping: A type of leaf attachment without a leafstalk in which the leaf base grasps the main stalk, partly surrounding the stalk at the point of attachment.

Clustered needles: A group of needles emanating from a central point, usually within a papery sheath, as in pine trees.

Compound leaf: A single leaf composed of at least 2 but usually not more than 20 leaflets growing along a single leafstalk, as in Smooth Sumac.

Cone: A cluster of woody scales encasing multiple nutlets or seeds and growing on a central stalk, as in conifer trees.

Cone scale: An individual overlapping projection, often woody, on a conifer cone, as in Ponderosa Pine. See *bract*.

Conifer: A type of tree that usually does not shed all of its leaves each autumn, such as pine or spruce.

Crooked: Off center or bent in form, not straight, as in a Black Locust trunk.

Deciduous: A type of tree that usually sheds all of its leaves each autumn, such as White Oak or Sugar Maple.

Disk: A flattened, disk-like fruit that contains a seed, as in the American Elm. See *samara*.

Double-toothed margin: A jagged or serrated leaf edge that is composed of two types of teeth, usually one small and one large, as in Siberian Elm.

Flower: To bloom, or produce a flower or flowers as a means of reproduction, as in deciduous trees.

Fruit: A ripened ovary or reproductive structure that contains one or more seeds, such as a nut or berry.

Furrowed: Having longitudinal channels or grooves, as in Bur Oak bark.

Gland: An organ or structure that secretes a substance, as in Nannyberry leafstalks.

Intolerant: Won't thrive in a particular condition, such as shade.

Lance-shaped: Long, narrow and pointed in form, like a spearhead, as in Weeping Willow leaves.

Leaf base: The area where a leafstalk attaches to the leaf.

Leaflet: One of the two or more leaf-like parts of a compound leaf, as in White Ash.

Leafstalk: The stalk of a leaf, extending from the leaf base to the branch. See *petiole*.

Lenticel: A small growth, usually on bark, that allows air into the interior of a tree, as in Paper Birch.

Lobed leaf: A single leaf with at least one indentation (sinus or notch) along an edge that does not reach the center or base of the leaf, as in oaks or maples.

Margin: The edge of a leaf.

Midrib: The central vein of a leaf, often more pronounced and larger in size than other veins, as in Black Cherry.

Naturalized: Not originally native, growing and reproducing in the wild freely now, such as Russian-olive.

Needle: A long, usually thin, evergreen leaf of a conifer tree.

Notch: A small indentation along the margin of a leaf, as in Red Maple.

Nut: A large fruit encased by hard walls, usually containing one seed, such as an acorn. See *fruit*.

Nutlet: A small or diminutive nut or seed, usually contained in a cone or cone-like seed catkin, as in Red Pine or Paper Birch. See *fruit*.

Opposite: A type of leaf attachment in which leaves are situated directly across from each other on a stalk, as in Sugar Maple.

Ovate: Shaped like an egg, as in Austrian Pine cones.

Palmate compound leaf: A single leaf that is composed of three or more leaflets emanating from a common central point at the end of the leafstalk, as in Ohio Buckeye.

Petiole: The stalk of a leaf. See *leafstalk*.

Petiolule: The stalk of a leaflet in a compound leaf.

Pitch pocket: A raised blister that contains a thick resinous sap, as in Balsam Fir bark.

Pith: The central soft part of a twig in a young branch, turning to hard wood when mature.

Pod: A dry fruit that contains many seeds and opens at maturity, as in Kentucky Coffeetree. See *capsule*.

Pollination: The transfer of pollen from the male anther to the female stigma, usually resulting in the production of seeds.

Rachis: The central or main stalk of a compound leaf, as in the European Mountain-ash.

Samara: A winged fruit that contains a seed, as in maples, ashes or elms. See *disk* and *fruit*.

Seed catkin: A small cone-like structure that contains nutlets or seeds, as in birches.

Sessile: Lacking a stalk and attaching directly at the base, as in Black Ash leaflets.

Simple leaf: A single leaf with an undivided or unlobed edge, as in American Elm.

Sinus: The recess or space in between two lobes of a leaf, as in the Red Oak.

Spine: A stiff, usually short, sharply pointed woody outgrowth from a branch or cone, as in Ponderosa Pine cones. See *thorn*.

Stalk: A thin structure that attaches a leaf, flower or fruit to a twig or branch.

Stipule: An appendage at the base of a stalk, usually small and in pairs, with one stipule on each side of stalk, as in Nannyberry.

Tannin: A bitter-tasting chemical found within acorns and other parts of a tree, as in oaks.

Terminal: Growing at the end of a stalk or branch.

Thorn: A stiff, usually long and sharply pointed woody outgrowth from a branch or trunk, as in Canada Plum. See *spine*.

Tolerant: Will thrive in a particular condition, such as shade.

Understory: A foliage layer that grows under a shady canopy of larger trees and which may include smaller tree species, such as Ironwood.

Whorl: A ring of three or more leaves, stalks or branches arising from a common point, as in Red Pine or Northern Catalpa.

Winged: A membranous, thin appendage, usually attached to a seed, as in maple seeds.

Woody: Composed of wood, as in trees or cones. See *cone scale*.

ABOUT THE AUTHOR:

Stan Tekiela is a naturalist, author and wildlife photographer with a Bachelor of Science degree in Natural History from the University of Minnesota. He has been a professional naturalist for over 20 years and is a member of the Minnesota Naturalist Association, the Outdoor Writers Association of America and Canon Professional Services. Stan actively studies and photographs trees, birds and wildflowers in the United States. He received an Excellence in Interpretation award from the National Association for Interpretation, and a regional award for Commitment to Outdoor Education. A columnist and radio personality, his syndicated column appears in more than 20 cities and he can be heard on a number of radio stations. Stan lives in Victoria, Minnesota, with wife Katherine and daughter Abigail. He can be contacted via his web page at www.naturesmart.com.

OTHER BOOKS BY STAN TEKIELA:

Birds of Minnesota Field Guide
Birds of Prey of Minnesota Field Guide
Wildflowers of Minnesota Field Guide

Trees of Michigan Field Guide
Birds of Michigan Field Guide
Wildflowers of Michigan Field Guide

Trees of Wisconsin Field Guide
Birds of Wisconsin Field Guide
Wildflowers of Wisconsin Field Guide

Nature Smart: A Family Guide to Nature
Start Mushrooming: The Easiest Way to Collect Edible Mushrooms